Teacher's Annotated Edition

Mathematics Workshop

Problem Solving 2

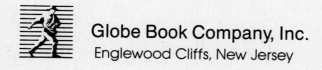

Globe Book Company, Inc.
Englewood Cliffs, New Jersey

Consultant

Dr. Alan Barson

Director, Chapter 1 Secondary Mathematics Program
City of Philadelphia
Philadelphia, Pennsylvania

Developed and produced for Globe Book Company by

Publicom, Inc.

ISBN: 1-55675-903-7 (Teacher's Annotated Edition)

PRINTED IN THE UNITED STATES OF AMERICA   2 3 4 5 6 7 8 9 0

To The Teacher

Problem Solving 1 and *Problem Solving 2* are part of the **Globe Mathematics Workshop** series. These two books are designed expressly to help students who are experiencing difficulty in problem solving in mathematics.

Difficulties in solving word problems rest largely in the areas of using reading skills and applying critical thinking skills.

Reading Skills: The instructional paragraphs and the problems in these two books are written at a controlled reading level, one that is well within the capabilities of most junior high school students achieving below grade level. Every new instructional concept is accompanied by an example, providing the student with an immediate application of the skill. In addition, the subject matter of the problems has been carefully selected to relate to students' everyday experiences. From the outset, students constantly use and check their reading comprehension skills. After reading each problem, they identify the question(s) being asked and then restate the question(s) in their own words.

Critical Thinking Skills: In following the problem solving steps outlined in these books, students come to develop and use both intellectual and decision-making critical thinking skills. *Intellectual skills,* such as classifying, interpreting, analyzing, summarizing, synthesizing, and evaluating information, are all used in finding information and selecting the relevant facts needed to solve a problem. *Decision-making skills* are used in eliminating nonrelevant information, in determining the correct mathematics operations, and in selecting the most suitable strategy (or strategies) for solving the problem.

Problem Solving 1 and *Problem Solving 2* may be used to supplement the problem solving sections of any basal mathematics program. They may also be used as a "stand-alone" program—either for students achieving below grade level or as a review of problem solving techniques for students of average ability.

Problem Solving 1 and Problem Solving 2

The two books in this series are self-contained. In *Problem Solving 1,* the pace of content coverage is carefully controlled, with considerable time devoted to cumulative practice of newly introduced skills and strategies.

Problem Solving 2 reintroduces and reinforces the problem solving skills and strategies developed in Book 1 at a faster pace and with new practice problems. Additional skills and strategies are introduced and applied to problems of a more complex nature. Book 2 concludes with the application of problem solving skills and strategies to problems that are found in practical, day-to-day situations.

The Five-Step Process

In *Problem Solving 1* and *Problem Solving 2,* the approach to solving all word problems is based on a five-step model. The "steps" in this model are as follows:

1. **Read the problem.** This first step helps the student to separate a problem into its two main parts—information and *the question being asked.* The ability to restate the question in a different form indicates that the student has identified and understood the question.

2. **Find the facts.** Once the question has been identified and understood, the student must decide what facts are needed to answer the question. The needed facts may be found "inside" or "outside" of the question. In some instances, the needed facts may not be obtainable, in which case that problem cannot be solved.

3. **Plan what to do.** At this step, the student must decide what strategy to use in order to answer the question. If an estimate of the answer can be made, it is made at this time.

4. **Carry out the plan.** This step represents the execution of the plan. It may be simply to perform one or more mathematics operations (addition, subtraction, multiplication, division), or it may be a *nonroutine* strategy.

5. **Check the answer.** Once a solution to a problem has been reached, it is critically examined during this step for reasonableness and accuracy.

In *Problem Solving 1,* this approach to problem solving is developed step-by-step until the entire model is complete. Thereafter, the model serves as a consistent framework for solving any word problem.

It is understood that many simple problems can be solved without going through all the steps of the model. However, students are encouraged to complete each discrete step, in order, for *every* problem they are asked to solve, regardless of its degree of difficulty. Such a disciplined approach to problem solving helps to reduce or eliminate the errors of omission or commission that so often occur as a result of hasty or disorganized problem solving techniques.

Organization and Features of the Books

Units

The content material in each book is divided into units. Book 1 is divided into three units based on the following: understanding the five-step model, developing the problem solving skills at each step, and learning more about problem solving strategies.

Book 2 is divided into four units. The first three units cover much of the same material as Units 1–3 of Book 1. However, Unit 1 is a *review* of the five-step model, while Units 2 and 3 *reinforce* and *extend* the skills and strategies developed in those same units in Book 1. Unit 4 deals with *applications* of problem solving skills and strategies to such everyday situations as balancing checkbooks and computing sales taxes.

Lessons

Each instructional lesson in these books is two pages in length and has an identical format. The format for each lesson is as follows:

Aim: This is a statement of the goal or objective of the lesson.

What You Need to Know: This section contains all of the information needed to reach the objective of the lesson.

Think About It: This section serves several purposes. First, it asks the student to answer one or two questions about the *What You Need to Know* section, "forcing" the student to stop and think about what was just read. This is followed by one or two Examples that apply or illustrate the point of the lesson. Usually in the form of sample problems, these Examples prepare the student for the *Practice* problems coming up. Concise explanations follow the Examples, helping to ensure that the student has understood the application of the lesson concept.

Practice: This section consists of several practice problems. These problems are similar to the samples used in the *Think About It* Examples.

The consistency of lesson length and format helps students become more comfortable with the content material. The fact that their responsibilities in each lesson are predictable makes the content seem less threatening.

Unit Reviews

Each unit is followed by a three-page *Unit Review.* Each *Unit Review* contains a variety of exercise types: true-false, sentence-completion, and multiple-choice items as well as problems for which the student demonstrates the use of all five problem solving steps in writing.

Additional Practice

For each lesson in the book, this section has a corresponding page of practice exercises. The page number is given at the end of each lesson in the student edition.

The exercises in this section provide flexibility to the program in that they can be utilized in a variety of ways. For example, they may be used as additional classroom work, as homework assignments, as extra credit or enrichment, or as evaluation aids. The way in which these exercises are used depends, to a large degree, on the ability of the students in your class and the pace at which they proceed through lessons.

Whole-Book Review

Each book in this series concludes with a *Whole-Book Review.* Problems in the *Whole-Book Review* are of the exercise type that concludes each *Unit Review,* namely, the type that requires the student actually to demonstrate his or her thinking during each of the five steps in the problem solving process. This review is designed to help you to evaluate student mastery of all the skills and concepts developed in the book.

Appendix

Each book has an *Appendix.* Obtaining information from an appendix is one of the skills developed in the course of this program. Thus, students will be required to refer to the *Appendix* in order to solve certain problems in each book.

Teaching the Lessons

Depending on your students' level of achievement, most of the lessons in these books may be completed in a single class period (not including the *Additional Practice* exercises). The following is one possible "timetable" for teaching the lessons in these books.

1. Read the lesson *Aim,* or have a student read it. Be sure that everyone understands what the lesson is about.

2. Lead students through the *What You Need to Know* section. Take as much time as necessary with this section. It contains the essential content of the lesson.

3. Have students read the question portion of the *Think About It* section. Once it has been determined that everyone understands the question(s), give students a few minutes to write their answer(s) to the question(s). Have students read their answers.

    Proceed to the Example(s) and the explanatory material that follows. Again, make sure that students understand what was done and why. The Examples are models of the exercises in the *Practice* section.

4. Have students start working on the exercises in the *Practice* section. Depending on your students' abilities and pace, you may have them—

a. complete the practice exercises, read their responses aloud, and discuss any questions. You may wish to assign problems from the *Additional Practice* page for homework.

b. work on the exercises until the end of the period and complete the *Practice* section for homework.

5. The next class period should begin with a review of the previous lesson. For more able students, this review may consist of going over the homework assignment. For students working at a slower pace, you may wish to spend the entire period going over the lesson, discussing homework, and working in class on problems from the *Additional Practice* page.

Using the Teacher's Annotations

In the Teacher's Annotated Editions of *Problem Solving 1* and *Problem Solving 2,* annotations are printed, in color, directly on the student pages. These annotations consist of the following:

Answers or responses to questions   In many cases, these consist of "suggested" or "acceptable" responses, since more than one correct response is frequently possible.

Teaching hints and suggestions   These consist of background information, alternative approaches to problems, suggested items for class discussion, and particular "trouble items" to watch for—items that frequently prove difficult for students.

As noted above, these annotations appear on the student pages in the Teacher's Annotated Editions; thus the information is available when and where it is needed.

A Note About Calculators

The use of hand-held calculators in the mathematics classroom is becoming widespread. In some schools, the use of calculators is required. Many of the exercises in these books lend themselves readily to the use of calculators. At numerous points throughout the Teacher's Annotated Editions, the suggested use of the calculator as a computational tool is offered as an annotation. Students learn that there are times when the execution of a plan is best done mentally or using paper and pencil, and there are times when the execution is best done with a calculator.

Teacher's Annotated Edition

Mathematics Workshop

Problem Solving 2

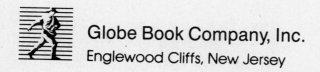
Globe Book Company, Inc.
Englewood Cliffs, New Jersey

Consultant

Dr. Alan Barson

Director, Chapter 1 Secondary Mathematics Program
City of Philadelphia
Philadelphia, Pennsylvania

Developed and produced for Globe Book Company by

Publicom, Inc.

Art and Photography Credits:

The illustrations were prepared by Judy Love.

The photographs were obtained from the following sources: Owen Franken/Stock, Boston, p. 1; Carol Palmer, pp. 17 and 61; Andrew Brilliant, p. 39.

Cover photo—Andrew Brilliant and Carol Palmer.

ISBN: 1-55675-903-7 (Teacher's Annotated Edition)
ISBN: 1-55675-902-9 (Student Edition)

PRINTED IN THE UNITED STATES OF AMERICA   2 3 4 5 6 7 8 9 0

Contents

Introductory Lesson

Aim: To review how lessons are organized in this program, and to review the five-step approach to solving word problems

What You Need to Know

The lessons in *Mathematics Workshop: Problem Solving* 2 have the same organization as the lessons in Book 1. If you have not done *Problem Solving 1,* check with your teacher to make sure you are in the right book.

Unit 1 in Book 2 is a review of Book 1. In Unit 1, you will review the five problem solving steps. In Units 2 and 3, you will practice the strategies learned in Book 1 for solving different types of problems. You will also learn some new strategies. In Unit 4, you will see just how important it is in everyday life to be able to solve problems.

As in Book 1, each lesson begins with an "Aim," telling you what you will learn in the lesson. This is followed by three major sections: "What You Need to Know," "Think About It," and "Practice."

Book 1 gave me the right key.

Think About It

Name three major ideas that this Introductory Lesson says you "need to know."

You need to know that Book 1 should be done before Book 2, that Book 2

reviews and extends Book 1, and that Book 2 is organized similarly to

Book 1.

You probably remember that the "Think About It" section always starts with a question. Like the question above, it is about something you read in the "What You Need to Know" section.

After the question, there are one or two Examples. The Examples are word problems. They show how to apply the new information. Also, they are similar to the Practice problems you will be doing in the third section of the lesson.

Example A How many units are in this book?
Answer: *There are 4 units.*

Example B The map shows the route Brad takes when he walks from his home to school each morning. How far does Brad walk to school?

Step 1 (Read, reread, and reword): *How many blocks from school does Brad live?*

Step 2 (Find the needed facts): *Blocks on Sharp Street: 4.5; blocks on Pointed Parkway: 3; blocks on Thorn Avenue: 5.25*

Step 3 (Plan what to do): *Add (blocks on Sharp + blocks on Pointed + blocks on Thorn = total number of blocks)*
    Sometimes, Step 3 also includes making an estimate: 5 + 3 + 5 = 13.

Step 4 (Carry out the plan):
$$\begin{array}{r} 4.50 \\ 3.00 \\ +\ 5.25 \\ \hline 12.75 \end{array}$$
Answer:
12.75 blocks

Step 5 (Check the answer): *Is answer reasonable? Yes. Does computation check? Yes. (In this case, you would add "backward": 5.25 + 3.00 + 4.50 = 12.75.)*

Both Examples apply what you are learning to a specific situation. Example B also gives you a brief review of the steps you learned in Book 1.

Remember from Book 1, after the Examples there is a paragraph. Like the one above, the paragraph says something more about the Examples.

Practice

The third section in each lesson is "Practice." This is where you show how well you have understood the lesson. If you have trouble with the problems in this section, study the first two sections again.

1. What does the first unit in Book 2 do? _It reviews the five problem_
   solving steps learned in Book 1.

2. After "Aim," what is the first section in each lesson called?
   "What You Need to Know"

3. In which section of the lesson are the Examples found?
   The Examples are in the "Think About It" section.

4. Show how you would **estimate** an answer to the following computations. Accept reasonable estimates.

   a. 110×9: _100_ $\times$ _10_ = _1,000_

   b. $198 \div 11$: _200_ $\div$ _10_ = _20_

5. Read this word problem. Use the map in Example B to answer the questions that follow.

   Barb rides the subway between school and home twice a day. How far does she ride the subway each day?

   a. What fact is needed from the map? _9.75 blocks_

   b. In this word problem, would a final answer of 3 blocks make sense? Why or why not?
      It would not make sense. How could Barb ride a shorter distance
      altogether than she rides one way?

As in Book 1, there is a Unit Review at the end of each unit in Book 2. Look at the Unit 1 Review on pages 14–16 to remind yourself about the types of questions that appear in a Unit Review.
   The following sections are found at the end of the book:

   - Additional Practice items for each lesson (pages 83–115)
   - Whole-Book Review (pages 116–119)
   - Appendix (pages 120–122)

Look at each of these sections. They should all seem familiar. They are similar to the sections at the end of *Problem Solving 1.* As you work through Book 2, you will find that your "keys" work better and better.

Step One: Read the Problem

Aim: To read a word problem and reword the question

What You Need to Know

All word problems have two main parts. They contain **information** and a **question**. In the information part, you find the facts that you will use to answer the question. Before you begin to solve a word problem, you must make sure you *understand the question.*

So, Step 1 in solving any word problem is to—

- READ the problem. Get a general picture of what the problem is about.
- REREAD the problem more slowly. Focus on the details.
- REWORD the question. Put the question in your own words.

Think About It

Why do you think it helps to reword the question in a word problem?

Rewording the question means you understand it and helps you to

remember it.

Read and reread the following word problems. Then notice how the question is restated for each.

Example A The seventh- and eighth-grade students at Morris Junior High started a computer club. Altogether, 26 students attended the first meeting. Four more seventh-grade students attended the meeting than eighth-grade students. How many seventh-grade students attended the first meeting?
The Question: *How many seventh-grade students attended the first meeting?*

Example B The club voted to charge each member $5.75 to cover the cost of supplies. If 17 members pay the first week, how much money will be added to the club treasury?
The Question: *How much money will be collected?*

In Example A, the question is restated exactly as it appears in the problem. In Example B, the question is **reworded.** Always try to reword the question. Rewording shows that you understand the meaning of the words in the problem.

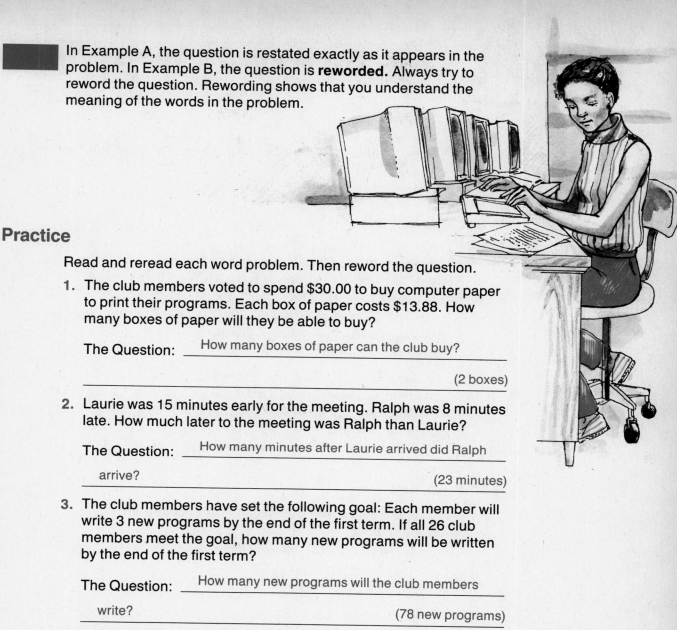

Practice

Read and reread each word problem. Then reword the question.

1. The club members voted to spend $30.00 to buy computer paper to print their programs. Each box of paper costs $13.88. How many boxes of paper will they be able to buy?

   The Question: _How many boxes of paper can the club buy?_

   _____ (2 boxes)

2. Laurie was 15 minutes early for the meeting. Ralph was 8 minutes late. How much later to the meeting was Ralph than Laurie?

   The Question: _How many minutes after Laurie arrived did Ralph_

   arrive? (23 minutes)

3. The club members have set the following goal: Each member will write 3 new programs by the end of the first term. If all 26 club members meet the goal, how many new programs will be written by the end of the first term?

   The Question: _How many new programs will the club members_

   write? (78 new programs)

4. Mark spent $16\frac{1}{2}$ hours writing his first program. Carla spent $12\frac{3}{4}$ hours writing her first program. How many more hours did Mark spend than Carla?

   The Question: _What is the difference in the number of hours Mark_

   and Carla spent writing their programs? ($3\frac{3}{4}$ more hours)

5. Club members can use the school computers between 2:30 and 4:00 on Monday and Wednesday afternoons. They can use the computers between 1:15 and 3:00 Tuesday, Thursday, and Friday afternoons. What is the total number of hours the members can use the computers in 1 week?

   The Question: _How many hours are the computers available to club_

   members in 1 week? (8.25 hours)

Teacher Note: Accept any degree of rewording as long as some rewording has occurred while retaining the meaning.

Although students are not asked to solve the Practice problems, many students will do so. Answers to the problems are included for your information.

Additional word problems for Lesson 1 skills practice are on page 83.

Step Two: Find the Facts

Aim: To find the facts needed to solve a word problem

What You Need to Know

In Step 1, you read and reread the problem and then reword the question. In Step 2, you look at the other main part of the word problem. You look at the information part. You FIND THE FACTS needed to answer the question.

Often, a word problem will have extra information—facts you do not need. Keep the question in mind at all times. Decide which of the facts are important.

Many times, you can find all the needed facts "inside" the problem. Other times, you will have to look for facts "outside" the problem. You might find data in a diagram, a chart, a map, an appendix, or a dictionary. It doesn't matter where you find the facts as long as they help you to answer the question.

Think About It

Name three places "outside" a word problem where you may find needed facts.

Students may list any three of these: a diagram, a chart, a map, an

appendix, a dictionary.

Read each word problem below. Notice both the question and the facts needed to solve the problem. The question is underlined.

Example A The annual crafts street fair is open from 9 A.M. to 5 P.M. on Saturday and from 1 P.M. to 6 P.M. on Sunday. How many hours is the fair open on Saturday?

The Facts: *Time fair opens on Saturday: 9 A.M.*
Time fair closes on Saturday: 5 P.M.

Example B Candy made clay creatures to sell at the street fair. Marie bought 2 bugs and 3 small dinosaurs. How much did Marie pay Candy?

The Facts: *Number of bugs: 2*
Price of bugs: $1.25
Number of small dinosaurs: 3
Price of small dinosaurs: $3.45

Candy's Clay Creatures	
bugs	$1.25
dogs, cats	$3.95
horses	$4.95
dinosaurs	
large	$5.75
small	$3.45

In Example A, all the needed facts are "inside" the problem. In Example B, some of the needed facts are "outside" the problem, in a chart. Each problem contains extra information, facts that are *not* needed to solve the problem.

Practice

Teacher Note: Although students are not asked to solve the Practice problems, the answers are included below for your information.

For each word problem, <u>underline</u> the question. Then write the facts you need to solve the problem. You may find the facts inside or outside the problem.

1. Molly made a hat for the street fair. To decorate the hat, she used 2.7 meters of pink ribbon, 1.5 meters of green ribbon, and 2.4 meters of white ribbon. <u>How many meters of ribbon did she use in all?</u>

   The Facts: <u>Meters of pink ribbon: 2.7; meters of green ribbon: 1.5;</u>

   <u>meters of white ribbon: 2.4</u>   (6.6 meters)

2. Frank drew a map to show Ben how to get to the fair. <u>If Ben follows the map, how many blocks will he travel to the fair?</u>

   The Facts: <u>Blocks on Maple St.: 2½; blocks on Elm Terrace: 4;</u>

   <u>blocks on Oak St.: 3½</u>   (10 blocks)

3. Roberto made 6 plant hangers for the fair. He used 7½ balls of blue cord and 72 beads. <u>How many balls of cord did he use for each plant hanger?</u>

   The Facts: <u>Number of balls of cord in all: 7½; number of plant hang-</u>

   <u>ers made: 6</u>   (1.25 balls of cord)

4. Rosa makes beaded necklaces. To make 1 of her best-selling necklaces, she needs 25 large black beads, 48 small black beads, and 24 silver beads. <u>How many silver beads will Rosa need to make 8 of her best-selling necklaces?</u>

   The Facts: <u>Number of silver beads for 1 necklace: 24; number of</u>

   <u>necklaces in all: 8</u>   (192 silver beads)

5. During the last hour of the fair, Candy sold 3 large dinosaurs to Ken for $4.50 each. <u>How much did Ken save over the original price of the large dinosaurs?</u> (Hint: Use the chart on page 4.)

   The Facts: <u>Original price of each large dinosaur: $5.75; price Ken</u>

   <u>paid for each large dinosaur: $4.50; number of dinosaurs Ken</u>

   <u>bought: 3</u>   ($3.75)

Ben's house

Maple St.

Elm Terrace

City Park

Oak St.

crafts
street fair

Additional word problems for Lesson 2 skills practice are on page 84.

Step Three: Plan What to Do

Aim: To plan how to solve a word problem and, when possible, to estimate the answer

What You Need to Know

Teacher Note: Point out to students that estimates are fairly simple when single operations are planned. One can estimate the answers to problems that require only addition, subtraction, multiplication, or division. One can estimate when more than one operation will be needed, though that is more difficult and may benefit from the use of paper and pencil or a calculator. One cannot estimate when certain diagrams and more unusual or complex strategies will be used.

Once you know the question and find the needed facts, you can decide how to use the facts. In Step 3, you PLAN WHAT TO DO. Picture, or **visualize,** what is happening in the problem. This will help you to decide how to solve it.

For many problems, you will just need to compute. You will add, subtract, multiply, or divide. For other problems, you will use a different strategy. You may need to make a diagram, a table, or a graph. You may need to write an equation or use a formula. You may need some other strategy.

Once you have a plan, **estimate** the answer if you can. An estimate will help you to judge whether or not the final answer, when you get it, makes sense.

Think About It

What will help you to choose a strategy for solving a problem?

Visualize, or picture, what is happening in the problem.

Read the problems below. The question is underlined. There are circles around the needed facts. There is a label for the plan, such as "Add," followed by a description in parentheses.

Example A At the library, 365 books were checked out on Monday. On Tuesday, 397 books were checked out. How many books were checked out on Monday and Tuesday?

The Plan: *Add (books checked out on Monday + books checked out on Tuesday = total books checked out on Monday and Tuesday)*

The Estimate: *350 + 400 = 750*

Example B Rob volunteered to make a bulletin-board display for Book Week. The bulletin board is $12\frac{1}{2}$ feet wide and $6\frac{1}{2}$ feet long. How many square feet of space does Rob have for his display?

The Plan: *Use a formula: A = lw (area = length × width)*

The Estimate: *6 × 13 = 78*

In Example A, addition is used to solve the problem. In Example B, the formula for the area of a rectangle is needed *(A = lw)*. Formulas are included in the Appendix, on pages 120–122.

Practice

For each word problem, underline the question. Circle the needed facts. Then write a plan for solving the problem. Estimate the answer, if possible.

1. Suppose an average book in the library is 0.02 meter thick. How many meters of shelf space are needed for all 14,650 books?

    The Plan: _Multiply (number of books x space for 1 book = space for all books)_

    The Estimate: _14,500 × 0.02 = 290_
    (Computed answer: 293 meters)

2. The city is planning to repaint the baseboards along each wall in the main reading room of the library. The room is 27 feet wide and 52 feet long. How many feet of baseboard will be painted?

    The Plan: _Use a formula: P = 21 + 2w (Perimeter = [2 × length] + [2 × width])_

    The Estimate: _(2 × 50) + (2 × 30) = 160_ (Computed Answer: 158 feet)

3. Ms. Garcia, the librarian, wants to buy a 15-volume set of science books and a 6-volume set of geography books. Each science book costs $24.95. Each geography book costs $32.75. How much will it cost to buy both complete sets of books? (Hint: Use two mathematical operations.)

    The Plan: _Multiply and add ([cost of one science book × number of science books] + [cost of one geography book × number of geography books] = total cost)_

    The Estimate: _(25 × 15) + (30 × 6) = 555_
    (Computed Answer: $570.75)

4. The city is planning to carpet the reference area of the library. The carpet costs $10.95 per square yard. The reference area is 9 yards by 4 yards. How much will it cost to carpet the reference area? (Hint: Use two steps.)

    The Plan: _Use a formula: A = lw; then multiply (number of square yards × price per square yard = total cost)_

    The Estimate: _(9 × 4) × 10 = 360_
    (Computed Answer: $394.20)

Additional word problems for Lesson 3 skills practice are on page 85.

Step Four: Carry Out the Plan

Aim: To carry out the plan for solving a word problem

What You Need to Know

In Step 3 of the problem solving process, you decide *how* to solve a word problem. In Step 4, you CARRY OUT THE PLAN.

Often, your plan, or **strategy,** for solving a problem will require computation. You can solve some problems mentally, in your head. For other problems, you will use paper and pencil or a calculator. Look at the numbers in each computation. Then decide which method will work best for you.

Think About It

Name three methods for computing a word problem.

Solve mentally; use paper and pencil; use a calculator.

Read each word problem below. Notice how each step is completed. Step 1 is shown by underlining the question. Step 2 is shown by circling the needed facts. Step 3 is shown by labeling the plan and making an estimate. Step 4 is shown by carrying out, or executing, the plan.

Example A Rosa and Juan were hiking in Twin Lakes Park. They hiked for $3\frac{1}{4}$ hours. They stopped $1\frac{1}{4}$ hours for lunch. Then they continued hiking for $1\frac{2}{3}$ hours more. For how many hours did Rosa and Juan actually hike?

The Plan: *Add*   **The Estimate:** $3 + 2 = 5$

The Execution: $3\frac{1}{4}$ $3\frac{3}{12}$ **Answer:** $4\frac{11}{12}$ *hours*
(Use paper $+ 1\frac{2}{3}$ $+ 1\frac{8}{12}$
and pencil.) $4\frac{11}{12}$

Example B Altogether, 100 adults, 100 children between the ages of 6 and 18, and 53 children under 6 entered the park. How much money was collected?

The Plan: *Multiply and add*

The Estimate: $(100 \times 2) + (100 \times 1) = 300$

The Execution: 2.25 1.25 225 **Answer:** *$350*
(Solve $\times 100$ $\times 100$ $+ 125$
mentally.) 225 125 350

Twin Lakes Admission

Adults	$2.25
Children	
6–18 yrs	$1.25
under 6	free

In Example A, the problem can be solved using paper and pencil. In Example B, the problem can be solved mentally. In both problems, an estimated answer is found before computing.

Practice

For each problem, do each step as in the Examples. Show your computations in the space to the right of each item.

Hikers Snack Bar

Hamburgers	$1.35
Peanuts	$0.45
Popcorn	$1.00
Fruit (apples, oranges, pears)	$0.75
Juice (orange, grapefruit, punch)	$0.85

Teacher Note: Discuss with students how well their estimates approximated their computed answers. (In word problems that use mental math, as in Practice items 2 and 5, the estimate and the solution are often the same.) Ask students if they remembered to show <u>units</u> with their final answers.

1. Julie and Marge stopped for a snack as they entered the park. Julie got a hamburger and an orange juice. Marje got popcorn and an apple. <u>What was the total bill?</u>

   The Plan: _____Add_____

   The Estimate: ___1 + 1 + 1 + 1 = 4___   Answer: ___$3.95___

   1. The Execution

   $$\begin{array}{r} 1.35 \\ .85 \\ 1.00 \\ + .15 \\ \hline 3.95 \end{array}$$

2. The owners of the Hikers Snack Bar are hoping to sell 100 hamburgers today. If they reach their goal, <u>how much money will they take in on the sale of hamburgers?</u>

   The Plan: ___Multiply___

   The Estimate: ___1.35 × 100 = 135___   Answer: ___$135.00___

   2. The Execution

   $$\begin{array}{r} 1.35 \\ \times\ 100 \\ \hline 135 \end{array}$$

3. There are $44\frac{3}{4}$ km of hiking trails in Twin Lakes Park. Cody hiked $10\frac{1}{4}$ km on Monday. He hiked $11\frac{3}{4}$ km on Tuesday and $14\frac{3}{4}$ km on Wednesday. How much farther did he hike on Wednesday than on Monday?

   The Plan: ___Subtract___

   The Estimate: ___15 − 10 = 5___   Answer: ___4.5 km___

   3. The Execution

   $$\begin{array}{r} 14\frac{3}{4} \\ -\ 10\frac{1}{4} \\ \hline 4\frac{2}{4} = 4\frac{1}{2} \end{array}$$

4. Abe, Rosita, Carrie, Dave, and Eric bought 12.5 kg of food to take on their hiking trip. Each person carried the same amount of food. <u>How much weight in food did each person carry?</u>

   The Plan: ___Divide___

   The Estimate: ___15 ÷ 5 = 3___   Answer: ___2.5 kg___

   4. The Execution

   $$5\overline{)12.5}\quad 2.5$$

Additional word problems for Lesson 4 skills practice are on page 86.

Step Five: Check the Answer

Aim: To check the answer to a word problem

What You Need to Know

It may be tempting to go through the first four steps, get an answer, and stop there. Don't give in to the temptation! Step 5 is a very important step. You need to CHECK THE ANSWER.

Checking the answer means two things. First, check that the answer is **reasonable.** (Does it make sense? Does it answer the question? Is it close to the estimate you made in Step 3?) Second, check for **computation accuracy.**

Think About It

Why, do you think, is Step 5 one of the most important steps?

Answers may vary somewhat. It would be silly to go through Steps 1–4

and then stay with an incorrect answer.

Read each problem below. Notice the check that is used to decide if the answer is correct.

Example A During a track meet, David ran the 100-yard dash in 10.6 seconds. Joshua ran the same distance in 9.8 seconds. How much faster was Joshua's time than David's time?

The Plan: *Subtract*　　**The Estimate:** *11 − 10 = 1*

The Execution:　*10.6*　　**Answer:** *0.9 second*
　　　　　　　　　− 9.8
　　　　　　　　　0.9

The Check: *Is answer reasonable? Yes.*
　　　　　Does computation check? No. (Computing "backward" shows 9.8 + 0.9 = 10.7, not 10.6.)

Example B During practice, Joyce ran the 100-yard dash twice. She ran it in 11.3 seconds and in 10.2 seconds. What was Joyce's average time during practice?

The Plan: *Add*　　**The Estimate:** *11 + 10 = 21*

The Execution:　*11.3*　　**Answer:** *21.5 seconds*
　　　　　　　　　+ 10.2
　　　　　　　　　21.5

The Check: *Is answer reasonable? No. (How can an average time be longer than any single time?)*

In Example A, the answer is reasonable. It makes sense; it answers the question; it is close to the estimate. However, the computation does not check. The correct answer is 0.8 second.

In Example B, the answer is not reasonable. Whether or not the computation checks, you need to reread the problem. You may need to choose a different plan. In Example B, the plan needs to be "Add and divide." The correct answer is 10.75 seconds.

Practice

For each problem, study how Steps 3 and 4 were done. Then show the two-part check to decide if the answer is correct. If it is not, correct it.

Teacher Note: Be sure that students understand how computation accuracy is checked by doing the computation backward. For instance, numbers can be added or multiplied in a different order. Division can be checked by multiplying the quotient by the divisor (e.g., 12 ÷ 3 = 4; 4 × 3 = 12). Accept reasonable computation checks shown by students in their answers to the Practice items.

1. During a 1-mile relay race, Pete ran the first lap in 84.6 seconds. Rosa ran the second lap in 93.4 seconds. Tom ran the third lap in 87.8 seconds. How long did it take them to run the mile?

The Plan: Add

The Execution:
$$
\begin{array}{r}
84.6 \\
93.4 \\
+\ 87.8 \\
\hline
268.8
\end{array}
$$

The Estimate: 85 + 90 + 90 = 265

Answer: 268.8 seconds, or 4 min. 48 sec.

The Check: _The answer is reasonable. The computation is wrong._

(87.8 + 93.4 + 84.6 = 265.8) Correct answer: 265.8 seconds or 4 min. 43 sec.

2. In two practices, Lynn pole-vaulted 9.6 feet and 10.7 feet. By how many feet did she better the height from the first to the second vault?

The Plan: Subtract

The Execution:
$$
\begin{array}{r}
10.7 \\
-\ 9.6 \\
\hline
20.3
\end{array}
$$

The Estimate: 11 − 10 = 1

Answer: 20.3 feet

The Check: _The answer is not reasonable. Check the computation._

(10.7 − 9.6 = 1.1) Correct answer: 1.1 feet.

3. Maria practiced for the track meet for $1\frac{1}{2}$ hours each on Monday, Wednesday, and Friday. She practiced for $2\frac{1}{4}$ hours each on Tuesday and Thursday. For how many hours did Maria practice in all?

The Plan: Multiply and add

The Execution:
$$
\begin{array}{ccc}
1\frac{1}{2} & 2\frac{1}{4} & 4\frac{1}{2} \\
\times\ 3 & \times\ 2 & +\ 4\frac{1}{2} \\
\hline
4\frac{1}{2} & 4\frac{1}{2} & 9
\end{array}
$$

The Estimate: 5 × 2 = 10

Answer: 9 hours

The Check: _The answer is reasonable. The computation checks._

Teacher Note: Discuss with students how the estimate in item 3 was done. A number between 1½ and 2¼ was multiplied by the total number of days.

Additional word problems for Lesson 5 skills practice are on page 87.

11

Cumulative Practice: Steps 1, 2, 3, 4, and 5

Aim: To practice with Steps 1, 2, 3, 4, and 5 in combination

What You Need to Know

To review the five steps for solving any word problem, look at the top of the next page. Like the best teacher you ever had, these steps will never steer you wrong. They are a guide to success.

You may find that you can already do some of the steps mentally, in your head. There's nothing wrong with that! Just be sure *never to skip a step.* Each one is important to getting the right answer.

Think About It

Think about your own work with word problems in this unit. Where have you been most likely to make a mistake? Which step helps you to stay on the right track?

Answers will vary. This is a good item for class discussion.

Read the Example. Notice how all five steps are followed.

Example For a woodworking project, Janice cut two pieces from a board. She cut off a $22\frac{3}{8}$-inch piece and a $10\frac{5}{8}$-inch piece. A 38-inch piece of board was left. How long was the board originally?

The Question Reworded: *How long was the board before she cut the pieces?* (Question is underlined.)

The Facts: *Board lengths: $22\frac{3}{8}$ inches, $10\frac{5}{8}$ inches, 38 inches* (Needed facts are circled.)

The Plan: *Add*   **The Estimate:** *20 + 10 + 40 = 70*

The Execution: $22\frac{3}{8}$ **Answer:** *71 inches*
$$10\frac{5}{8}$$
$$\underline{+\ 38}$$
$$71$$

The Check: *Answer is reasonable.* (It answers the question, makes sense, and is close to the estimate.)
   Computation is correct. (Adding the numbers in a different order gives the same answer.)

The Example serves as a review of the five-step process for solving word problems. Be sure you have thought through the Example carefully before doing the Practice items below.

Practice

For each problem below, <u>underline</u> the question and ⃝circle the needed facts. Then write the plan and estimate the answer. Finally, carry out the plan and check the answer.

1. Mia's new car gets ⃝47.5 km per gallon for highway driving. It gets 33.1 km per gallon for city driving. <u>How many gallons of gas will Mia need to travel ⃝380 highway kilometers?</u>

   The Plan: _Divide_   The Estimate: _400 ÷ 50 = 8_

   The Answer: _8 gallons_   The Check: _The answer is reasonable._
   The computation is correct.

   1. The Execution

   $$47.5\overline{)380}\quad 8$$

2. Luiz bought ⃝2.5 pounds of ground meat that sold for ⃝$1.96 a pound. <u>How much did the ground meat cost?</u>

   The Plan: _Multiply_   The Estimate: _2.5 × 2 = 5_

   The Answer: _$4.90_   The Check: _The answer is reasonable._
   The computation is correct.

   2. The Execution

   $$\begin{array}{r} 1.96 \\ \times\ 2.5 \\ \hline 4.90 \end{array}$$

3. Beth bought a camera for ⃝$57.95 She bought ⃝2 rolls of film for ⃝$3.89 each. <u>What was her total bill?</u>

   The Plan: _Add_   The Estimate: _60 + 4 + 4 = 68_

   The Answer: _$65.73_   The Check: _The answer is reasonable._
   The computation is correct.

   3. The Execution

   $$\begin{array}{r} 57.95 \\ 3.89 \\ +\ 3.89 \\ \hline 65.73 \end{array}$$

4. A local TV station begins the day with a ⃝45-minute program of news and health tips. The news takes ⃝$11\frac{1}{2}$ minutes. <u>How much time is left for health tips?</u>

   The Plan: _Subtract_   The Estimate: _45 − 10 = 35_

   The Answer: _33½ minutes_ The Check: _The answer is reasonable._
   The computation is correct.

   4. The Execution

   $$\begin{array}{r} 45 \\ -\ 11\frac{1}{2} \\ \hline 33\frac{1}{2} \end{array}$$

Additional word problems for Lesson 6 skills practice are on page 88.

13

Unit 1 Review

A. On each line, write **T** or **F** to tell whether the statement is true or false.

T   **1.** Before you begin to solve a word problem, you must make sure you understand the question.

F   **2.** If you can reword the question in a word problem, it means you have solved the problem.

F   **3.** The facts needed to solve a word problem are always found "inside" the words of the problem.

T   **4.** Sometimes a word problem has extra information—facts that are not needed to solve the problem.

T   **5.** Visualizing what is happening in a problem may help you to decide how to solve the problem.

F   **6.** All you need to know to solve any word problem is how to add, subtract, multiply, or divide.

T   **7.** The plan for solving a word problem is called a *strategy*.

F   **8.** Using a calculator is the best method for solving all word problems.

T   **9.** When checking an answer, you should first check that the answer is reasonable and then check that the computation is accurate.

F   **10.** As a general rule, it is okay to skip a problem solving step to save time.

B. On each line, write the word that best completes the sentence.

question   **11.** The two main parts of any word problem are information and a ____.

facts   **12.** In Step 2 of the problem solving process, you find the ____ you need to answer the question.

estimate   **13.** Once you have a plan for solving a problem, it is a good idea to ____ the answer; this will help you judge whether the final answer, when you get it, makes sense.

carry out (or execute)   **14.** After you decide how to solve a word problem, you are ready to ____ the plan.

check   **15.** The last step in solving any word problem is to ____ the answer.

C. Circle the letter of the correct answer.

Kevin is learning to play the guitar. His brother plays the piano. A guitar lesson is $\frac{1}{2}$ hour long and costs $7.25. A book of music costs $3.95. How much does Kevin pay for 5 guitar lessons?

16. Which of these is a rewording of the question in the problem above?
    a. How much do 5 books of music cost?
    b. How much more does a guitar lesson cost than a book of music?
    c. How much does it cost Kevin for 5 guitar lessons?
    d. How much do a guitar lesson and a book of music cost?

17. Which of these is a needed fact for solving the problem above?
    a. A book of music costs $3.95.
    b. Guitar lessons cost $7.25 each.
    c. A guitar lesson lasts $\frac{1}{2}$ hour.
    d. Kevin's brother takes piano lessons.

18. Which of these is a plan for solving the word problem above?
    a. Add (price of guitar lesson + price of book)
    b. Multiply (5 × price of books)
    c. Subtract (price of guitar lessons − price of book)
    d. Multiply (5 × price of guitar lesson)

19. Which of these shows a way to estimate the answer to the problem above?
    a. 5 × 7 = 35   b. 5 × 4 = 20   c. 7 − 4 = 3   d. 7 + 4 = 11

20. To decorate a costume, Amy used $3\frac{3}{4}$ yards of blue ribbon and $2\frac{1}{2}$ yards of yellow ribbon. How much ribbon did she use in all?
    a. $6\frac{1}{4}$ yards   b. $5\frac{1}{4}$ yards   c. $5\frac{4}{6}$ yards   d. $6\frac{1}{2}$ yards

21. Wendy drove 418 miles on Monday and 279 miles on Tuesday. How much farther did she drive on Monday than on Tuesday?
    a. 697 miles   b. 261 miles   c. 139 miles   d. 249 miles

22. Todd bought 3 cans of tennis balls. The total bill was $8.37. How much did he pay for each can of tennis balls?
    a. $0.28   b. $25.11   c. $27.90   d. $2.79

There are 28 students in Ms. Went's class. Each student is writing a 9-page science report. How many pages will Ms. Went have to read?

23. Which of these is NOT a reasonable answer to the problem above?
    a. 262 pages   b. 625 pages   c. 252 pages   d. 272 pages

24. Which of these is the correct answer to the problem above?
    a. 262 pages   b. 625 pages   c. 252 pages   d. 272 pages

25. Which of these shows a way to check the computation for the problem above?
    a. 252   b. 28   c. 28   d. 9)252
       − 28   + 9   − 9

D. Read and reread each word problem. Then follow the directions to show your solution to the problem.

Dawn's apartment   library

6 km

3.5 km

5.8 km   3.3 km

Food Mart   Tracy's apartment

26. From her apartment, Dawn roller-skated past the Food Mart to Tracy's apartment. <u>How many kilometers did she skate in all?</u>

   a. Underline the question.

   b. Circle the needed facts in the problem.

   c. Describe your plan: _Add (kilometers from Dawn's apartment to Food_

     Mart + kilometers from Food Mart to Tracy's apartment = total kilometers)

   d. If an estimate can be made, show it here: _6 + 3 = 9_

   e. Carry out your plan. Answer: _9.1 km_   (5.8 + 3.3 = 9.1)

   f. Check your answer. If you got an incorrect answer, tell how you know it is wrong. Then write the correct answer.

     Students who got incorrect answers should mention computation error or

     that the answer was not reasonable.

27. The school football team is buying (12 new helmets) and 8 new footballs. Helmets cost (\$89 each,) and footballs cost \$35 each. <u>How much will the team spend on new helmets?</u>

   a. Underline the question.

   b. Circle the needed facts in the problem.

   c. Describe your plan: _Multiply (number of helmets × price of one helmet_

     = total cost)

   d. If an estimate can be made, show it here: _10 × 90 = 900_

   e. Carry out your plan. Answer: _\$1,068_   (89 × 12 = 1,068)

   f. Check your answer. If you got an incorrect answer, tell how you know it is wrong. Then write the correct answer.

     Students who got incorrect answers should mention computation error or

     that the answer was not reasonable.

2 Developing Your Problem Solving Skills

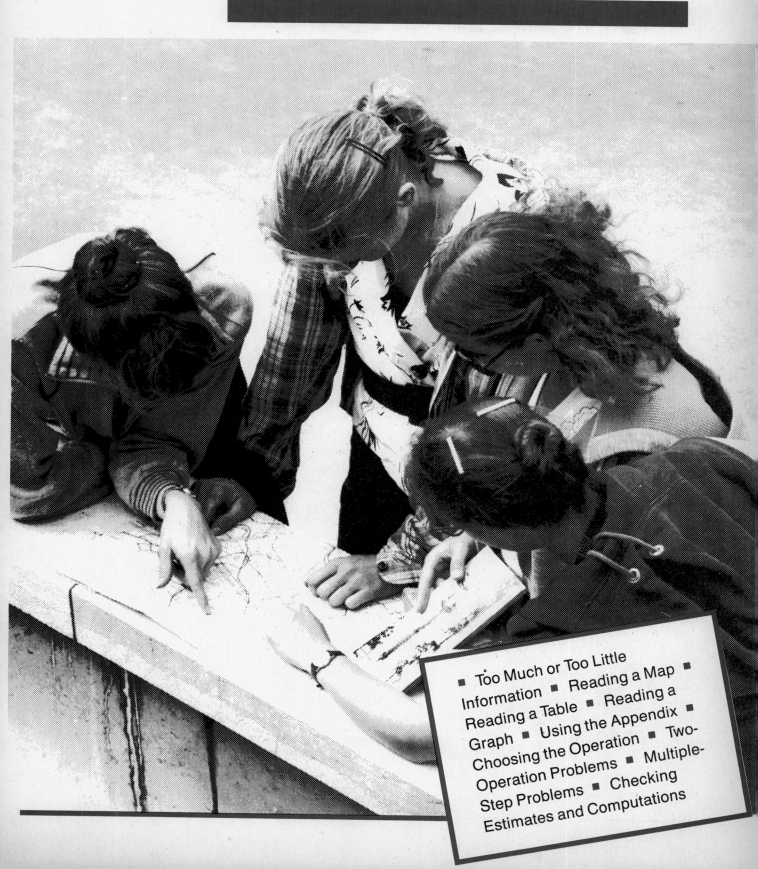

- Too Much or Too Little Information ▪ Reading a Map ▪ Reading a Table ▪ Reading a Graph ▪ Using the Appendix ▪ Choosing the Operation ▪ Two-Operation Problems ▪ Multiple-Step Problems ▪ Checking Estimates and Computations

Too Much or Too Little Information

Aim: To recognize when a problem contains unneeded facts or not enough facts

What You Need to Know

Problems in your daily life will rarely come with just the right amount of information. Often, there are extra, unimportant facts that you do not need to solve the problem. Other times, there may be too few facts to solve the problem.

Remember, your first task when solving any word problem is to be sure you *understand the question.* Then decide what facts you need to solve the problem. You may need to look both "inside" and "outside" the problem for the facts. Ask yourself, "Which of the given facts are needed to solve the problem? Are any important facts missing?" To solve the problem, you must have all the needed facts.

Think About It

When solving any word problem, what must you do before you can decide what facts you need?

Make sure you understand the question.

Read the word problems below. Notice the needed data. In each problem, there are circles around the important facts. The unnecessary facts are crossed out. If there is a missing fact, it is described.

Example A A tray holds (60 cookies) and a plate holds ~~24 cookies~~. If there are (5 trays) of cookies, how many cookies are on trays?

Missing Fact: *None*

The Execution: 60

        × 5

        300

Answer: *300 cookies*

grapes	($1.29/lb.)
pears	~~$0.79/lb.~~
bananas	~~$0.95/lb.~~

Example B Grapes, pears, and bananas are sold by the pound at Ace's Supermarket. Betty bought a bag of grapes. How much did she pay for the bag of grapes?

Missing Fact: *Number of pounds of grapes in the bag*

The Execution: *The problem cannot be solved.*

In Example A, there is one unneeded fact. You don't need to know how many cookies a plate will hold. That unnecessary fact is crossed out. There are no missing facts in the problem, so the problem can be solved.

In Example B, there is both unneeded information (the price per pound for pears and bananas) and missing information. To solve the problem, you would need to know how many pounds of grapes were in the bag. This problem cannot be solved with the facts given.

Teacher Note: After students have completed the Practice items, you may wish to have them supply sensible facts for problems 2 and 3 and then solve those problems.

Practice

For each problem, underline the question and reword it to yourself. Circle the needed data. Cross out the unnecessary data. If all the needed facts are given, solve the problem. If there is a missing fact, describe it as was done in Example B.

1. Lori is practicing for the track team. Each Tuesday, Thursday, and Saturday, she jogs $1\frac{1}{2}$ miles and does 25 leg lifts. On Monday, Wednesday, and Friday, she jogs $2\frac{1}{2}$ miles. How many leg lifts does Lori do in a week?

   75 leg lifts $(25 \times 3 = 75)$

2. Sailing classes are held Monday and Thursday afternoon. If both classes are full, how many people are taking sailing lessons?

   Missing fact: number of people in each sailing class

3. In the local library, $\frac{2}{5}$ of the books are nonfiction and $\frac{3}{5}$ of the books are fiction. How many fiction books are in the library?

   Missing fact: total number of books in the library

4. Luiz and Franco went fishing for 4 hours. They caught 5 bass and 6 catfish. Each catfish weighed 3 pounds. How many pounds of catfish did they catch?

   18 pounds $(6 \times 3 = 18)$

5. In a swimming relay, Karla swam her lap in 45.4 seconds. Joe swam his lap in 42.6 seconds. Kim swam her lap in 39.7 seconds. How much faster did Kim swim than Karla?

   5.7 seconds $(45.4 - 39.7 = 5.7)$

Reading a Map

Aim: To locate needed facts on a map

What You Need to Know

Sometimes the facts you need to solve a problem are found in a map. When you need to find data on a map, first study the *whole* map. Get an overall idea of what is included. Read the title of the map. Notice the kinds of places marked on the map. Find out how distances are shown on the map.

When you are solving a problem with a map, do the following:

- First, read the problem and understand the question.
- Second, study the map.
- Third, reread the problem while you locate the needed facts on the map.

Driving Distances between California Cities

(All distances are in miles.)

Think About It

Why should you study the whole map before trying to find the needed facts?

You will be less likely to miss a fact or use an unnecessary fact.

Read the word problems below. Notice where the facts needed to solve the problem are located.

Example A Carlos drove from San Francisco through Fresno to Bakersfield. How many miles did he drive?

Needed Map Facts: *187 miles, 104 miles*

The Execution:
$$\begin{array}{r} 187 \\ +\ 104 \\ \hline 291 \end{array}$$

Answer: *291 miles*

Example B Joan made 2 round trips from San Francisco to Crescent City last month. How many miles did she drive on these trips?

Needed Map Facts: *371 miles*

The Execution:
$$\begin{array}{r} 371 \\ \times\ 4 \\ \hline 1{,}484 \end{array}$$

Answer: *1,484 miles*

In both Examples A and B, the data needed to solve the problems are on the map. In Example B, there is also a piece of data "inside" the word problem. It tells you that Joan made "2 round trips." Each round trip would include a 371-mile trip from San Francisco to Crescent City *and* a 371-mile return trip from Crescent City back to San Francisco. Therefore, Joan would make four 371-mile trips in all.

Practice

For each problem, write the facts you will use from the map. Write the plan and the answer. (Remember to follow all five steps!) Use the map on page 20 for items 1 and 2.

1. How much farther is it from Los Angeles to San Diego than it is from Los Angeles to Santa Barbara? Use the shortest distances possible.

   Needed Map Facts: _____ 118 miles; 95 miles _____

   The Plan: __Subtract__   Answer: __23 miles__

   (118 = 95 = 23)

2. It took Juan 4 hours to drive from San Francisco to Paso Robles. He drove the same number of miles each hour. How many miles did Juan drive each hour?

   Needed Map Facts: _____ 202 miles _____

   The Plan: __Divide__   Answer: __50½ miles__

   ($202 \div 4 = 50\frac{1}{2}$)

Driving Distances between Tennessee and North Carolina Cities
(All distances are in miles.)

3. Billy drove from his home in Asheville through Charlotte to Greensboro. How many miles did he drive in all?

   Needed Map Facts: _____ 113 miles; 94 miles _____

   The Plan: __Add__   Answer: __207 miles__

   (113 + 94 = 207)

4. Julie drove from Memphis through Nashville to Chattanooga. Debbie drove the shortest route from Memphis to Chattanooga. How many more miles did Julie drive than Debbie?

   Needed Map Facts: _____ 87 miles; 132 miles; 133 miles; 320 miles _____

   The Plan: __Add and subtract__   Answer: __32 more miles__

   (87 + 132 + 133 = 352; 352 − 320 = 32)

Additional word problems for Lesson 8 skills practice are on page 90.

Reading a Table

What You Need to Know

 A table organizes all the numbers you see on bus, train, and airline **schedules.** With a table, you can find pieces of information quickly. The first thing to do is read the title and any headings. These will give you an overall understanding. Then look for the facts you need.

Think About It

Read the title and heading in the table below. Where does the 6:10 A.M. train from Cedarton stop before reaching Oaksbury?

It stops at Appleville and Wilson.

Read the Examples. Notice where the needed facts are found.

Commuter Train Schedule							
Cedarton to Oaksbury				**Oaksbury to Cedarton**			
Departs			**Arrives**	**Departs**	**Arrives**		
Cedarton	Appleville	Wilson	Oaksbury	Oaksbury	Wilson	Appleville	Cedarton
6:10 A.M.	6:15 A.M.	6.25 A.M.	6.57 A.M.	9:30 A.M.	10:03 A.M.	10.13 A.M.	10:18 A.M.
7:10 A.M.	—	7:22 A.M.	7:54 A.M.	11:45 A.M.	—	12:25 P. M.	12:30 P. M.
8:30 A.M.	8:35 A.M.	8:45 P. M.	9:17 A.M.	3:20 P. M.	3:53 P. M.	4:03 P. M.	4:08 P. M.
11:20 A.M.	11:25 A.M.	—	12:04 P. M.	5:10 P. M.	5:43 P. M.	5:53 P. M.	5:58 P. M.
3.15 P. M.	3:20 P. M.	3:40 P. M.	4:12 P. M.	6:20 P. M.	6:53 P. M.	7:03 P. M.	7:08 P. M.
6:30 P. M.	6:35 P. M.	6:45 P. M.	7:17 P. M.	6:45 P. M.	7:18 P. M.	—	7:30 P. M.
8:45 P. M.	8:50 P. M.	9:00 P. M.	9:32 P. M.	8:10 P. M.	8:43 P. M.	8:53 P. M.	8:58 P. M.

Example A Amy commutes to work by train from Cedarton to Oaksbury every day. If she rides the 7:10 A.M. train, how long does it take her to get to Oaksbury?

Needed Table Facts: *7:10 A.M.; 7:54 A.M.*

The Execution: *7 hr. 54 min.*   **Answer:** *44 minutes*
    − 7 hr. 10 min.
    44 min.

Example B Amy takes the 6:20 P.M. train home from Oaksbury to Cedarton. After leaving the train, she still has a 12-minute walk. What time does she get home?

Needed Table Facts: *7:08 P.M.*

The Execution: *7 hr.   8 min.*   **Answer:** *7:20 P.M.*
    + 12 min.
    7 hr. 20 min.

For Example A, look for the train that leaves Cedarton at 7:10 A.M.
For Example B, look for the train leaving Oaksbury at 6:20 P.M.

Practice

Write the facts you will use from the table. Then write the plan and
the answer. Use the schedule on page 22 for items 1, 2, and 3.

1. Blanca took the 5:10 P.M. train from Oaksbury to Appleville. How
   long was her train ride?

   Needed Table Facts: _____5:53 P.M._____

   The Plan: ___Subtract___ Answer: ___43 minutes___
   (5 hr. 53 min. − 5 hr. 10 min. = 43 min.)

2. One morning, the 7:10 A.M. train from Cedarton was 15 minutes
   late arriving at Oaksbury. What time did it get there?

   Needed Table Facts: _____7:54 A.M._____

   The Plan: ___Add___ Answer: ___8:09 A.M.___
   (7 hr. 54 min. + 15 min. = 8 hr. 9 min.)

3. Dave rides to work on the 6:25 A.M. train from Wilson to Oaksbury 5 days a week. How much time does he spend commuting to
   work on the train in 1 week?

   Needed Table Facts: _____6:57 A.M._____

   The Plan: ___Subtract and___ Answer: ___160 min., or 2 hr. 40 min.___
   ___multiply___ (6 hr. 57 min. − 6 hr. 25 min. = 32 min; 5 × 32 = 160)

North-Bound Bus Schedule							
Leave		So. County					**Arrive**
North Port	Englewood	Courthouse Annex	Venice Hospital	Venice	Nokomis	Osprey	Sarasota Sq. Mall
7:15 A.M.	7:35 A.M.	7:50 A.M.	8:00 A.M.	8:05 A.M.	8:10 A.M.	8:15 A.M.	8:25 A.M.
9:45 A.M.	10:05 A.M.	10:20 A.M.	10:30 A.M.	10:35 A.M.	10:40 A.M.	10:45 A.M.	10:55 A.M.
12:45 P.M.	1:05 P.M.	1:20 P.M.	1:30 P.M.	1:35 P.M.	1:40 P.M.	1:45 P.M.	1:55 P.M.
3:15 P.M.	3:35 P.M.	3:50 P.M.	4:00 P.M.	4:05 P.M.	4:10 P.M.	4:15 P.M.	4:25 P.M.
5:45 P.M.	6:05 P.M.	6:20 P.M.	6:30 P.M.	6:35 P.M.	6:40 P.M.	6:50 P.M.	6:55 P.M.
—	—	—	—	7:20 P.M.	7:25 P.M.	7:30 P.M.	7:35 P.M.

4. Nathan caught the 10:30 A.M. bus at Venice Hospital and rode to
   Sarasota Square Mall. How long was his bus ride?

   Needed Table Facts: _____10:55 A.M._____

   The Plan: ___Subtract___ Answer: ___25 min.___
   (10 hr. 55 min. − 10 hr. 30 min. = 25 min.)

5. The bus that leaves North Port at 5:45 P.M. was 23 minutes late
   arriving at Osprey. What time did the bus arrive at Osprey?

   Needed Table Facts: _____6:50 P.M._____

   The Plan: ___Add___ Answer: ___7:13 P.M.___
   (6 hr. 50 min. + 23 min. = 7 hr. 13 min.)

Additional word problems for Lesson 9 skills practice are on page 91.

Reading a Graph

What You Need to Know

Sometimes you will find needed facts in a graph. A **line graph** can show change over time. If there is a *trend* (a steady increase, decrease, or period of no change), this can be seen easily. The steeper the line, the sharper the increase or decrease.

Read the title and all labels on a graph before you begin to look for specific data. Be sure you understand the *intervals,* or units, that are used along both scales of the graph.

Think About It

Read the labels on the graph on this page. What do the numbers along the left side of the graph represent? _____temperatures (°F)_____

What is shown along the bottom of the graph? _____months_____

Read the Example below. Notice where the facts are found.

Example

Monthly Normal Temperatures
Boston, Massachusetts

How many degrees warmer is the monthly normal temperature in Boston in July than in January?
Needed Graph Facts: *74 degrees; 30 degrees*

The Execution: 74   **Answer:** *44 degrees*
                   − 30
                   ————
                    44

In the Example, the needed facts are found in the line graph. Notice that the line from January to February goes almost straight across. This shows that the normal temperature is about the same (30–31°F) for these two months. The line goes up steeply from February to July. This shows a sharp *increase* in the normal temperature. The line goes down from July to December. This shows a *decrease* in the normal temperature.

Practice

For each problem, write the facts you will use from the graph. Then write the plan and the answer. (Follow all five problem solving steps.) Use the graph on page 24 for items 1 and 2.

1. In Boston, how many degrees colder is the normal temperature in March than in April?

   Needed Graph Facts: _____38°F; 49°F_____

   The Plan: ___Subtract___   Answer: ___11 degrees___

   (49 − 38 = 11)

2. One day in August, the temperature went 13 degrees above normal for August. How high did the temperature go on that day?

   Needed Graph Facts: _____72°F_____

   The Plan: ___Add___   Answer: ___85°F___

   (80 + 13 = 93)

Daily High and Low Temperatures

3. How many degrees warmer was the high temperature on Wednesday than the high temperature on Monday?

   Needed Graph Facts: _____83°F; 74°F_____

   The Plan: ___Subtract___   Answer: ___9 degrees___

   (83 − 74 = 9)

4. Forecasters are predicting that the high temperature on Saturday will be 6 degrees higher than the high temperature on Friday. What is the high temperature on Saturday predicted to be?

   Needed Graph Facts: _____78°F_____

   The Plan: ___Add___   Answer: ___84°F___

   (78 + 6 = 84)

Additional word problems for Lesson 10 skills practice are on page 92.

Lesson 11

Using the Appendix

Aim: To locate needed facts in an appendix

What You Need to Know

Sometimes, needed facts are not only "outside" the problem—they're not even on the problem page! When this happens, ask yourself, "Where can I find that fact?" Remember, it doesn't matter *where* you find it, as long as you find it.

The fact you need may be on a calendar, in an almanac, in a dictionary, or on another page in your math book. To solve the problems in this lesson, you will find needed data in the Appendix, on pages 120–122.

Think About It

Name the types of facts that are found in this book's Appendix.

The Appendix includes metric and customary measures, time measure,

an Operations Chart, and formulas.

Read the problems below. Check the Appendix for each problem to see where the data are found.

Example A A nail weighs about 2 grams. About how many nails are in a bag that weighs 1 kilogram?
Needed Appendix Facts: *1 kg = 1,000 g*
The Execution: $\frac{500}{2)\,1,000}$ **Answer:** *about 500 nails*

height

base

Example B Find the area of a triangle with a base of 8 cm and a height of 5 cm.
Needed Appendix Facts: $A = \frac{1}{2}bh$
The Execution: $\frac{1}{2} \times 8 \times 5 = 20$ **Answer:** *20 cm²*

The facts needed to solve both Examples A and B can be found in the Appendix. In Example A, you need to convert kilograms to grams. In Example B, you need to find the formula for the area of a triangle.

Teacher Note: If necessary, review with students the use of geometric formulas to find perimeter, circumference, and area. These were used in Book 1 of *Unlocking Problem Solving*. In addition, the Appendix here in Book 2 includes the formula for finding the volume of a rectangular prism, a fact needed to solve Practice item 4.

Practice

For each problem, write the facts you will use from the Appendix. Then write the plan and the answer. Use 3.14 for π. Remember to follow all five problem solving steps, including the check on your answer.

1. The diameter of a bicycle wheel is 52 centimeters. What is the circumference of this bicycle wheel?

    Needed Appendix Facts: _____ $C = \pi d$ _____

    Answer: _____ 163.28 cm _____ $(3.14 \times 52 = 163.28)$

2. A developer owns $2\frac{1}{2}$ square miles of land. How many acres does she own?

    Needed Appendix Facts: _____ 1 square mile = 640 acres _____

    Answer: _____ 1,600 acres _____ $(640 \times 2.5 = 1,600)$

3. Ralph is carpeting his living room and dining room. He needs 182 square feet of carpet for the living room. He needs 106 square feet of carpet for the dining room. How many square yards of carpet does he need in all?

    Needed Appendix Facts: _____ 1 square yard = 9 square feet _____

    Answer: _____ 32 sq. yd. _____ $(182 + 106 = 288; 288 \div 9 = 32)$

4. This aquarium is a rectangular prism. Find its volume.

    Needed Appendix Facts: _____ $V = lwh$ _____

    Answer: _____ 46,332 cm³ _____ $(33 \times 52 \times 27 = 46,332)$

5. A truck carrying 6 metric tons of freight made deliveries to 4 warehouses. Each warehouse received the same amount of freight. How many kilograms of freight did each warehouse receive?

    Needed Appendix Facts: _____ 1 metric ton = 1,000 kg _____

    Answer: _____ 1,500 kg _____ $(6 \times 1,000 = 6,000; 6,000 \div 4 = 1,500)$

Choosing the Operation

Aim: To understand when to add, subtract, multiply, or divide to solve a word problem

What You Need to Know

Many word problems are *routine*. You simply add, subtract, multiply, or divide to solve them. To choose the operation, *visualize* the action. Study the chart below.

Once you know the operation, then choose the best way to compute. The best way may be mentally, with paper and pencil, or with a calculator. Remember to estimate your answer first.

Choose the Operation

Action	Operation
Joining different-sized groups (a different number in each group) to find a total	Addition
Separating Objects to find a group that is left or **Comparing two groups** to find the difference	Subtraction
Joining equal groups to find a total	Multiplication
Sharing equally to find the size of each group or **Making groups of a given size** to find the number of groups	Division

Think About It

Why is it a good idea to estimate an answer before computing it?

The estimate is one check on the computed answer.

Read each problem below. Visualize the action.

Example A   There are 231 students going by bus to the Natural History Museum. Each bus holds 66 people. How many buses are needed?

The Action: *Making groups of a given size*

The Execution: $66\overline{)231}$ with $3\frac{1}{2}$ **Answer:** *4 buses*

Example B   At the museum gift shop, Marie bought a book for $2.95 and a pin for $1.79. How much did she spend in all?

The Action: *Joining different-sized groups*

The Execution:
$$\begin{array}{r} 2.95 \\ + 1.79 \\ \hline 4.74 \end{array}$$ **Answer:** *$4.74*

After "The Action" heading in each Example, a short version of the whole section from the chart is listed. Notice that the answer in Example A is $3\frac{1}{2}$. It is not possible to hire half a bus. The quotient must be rounded up, to 4.

Remember, when you have a **remainder** in the quotient, you need to decide how to "show" it in your answer. Read the problem again. Decide how to **interpret** the remainder. Show the computed mixed-number answer. Or, show the quotient rounded up or down to the next whole number. Or, show the remainder by itself.

Teacher Note: Review with students the above information about interpreting remainders in their answers. Be sure students understand that there are four ways to interpret a remainder and that which way is chosen depends on the question in the word problem.

Practice

For each problem, visualize the action. Then write the action, the operation, and the answer. (Be sure to check your answers. Do they agree with your estimates? Do they make sense?)

1. Going to the museum, the bus driver followed a route that was 17.5 km and took 25 minutes. On the way back, the driver took a route that was 15.9 km and took 20 minutes. How much farther was the trip to the museum than from the museum?

   The Action: _____Comparing two groups_____

   The Operation: ___Subtraction___ Answer: ___1.6 km___
   $(17.5 - 15.9 = 1.6)$

2. The museum takes $7\frac{1}{2}$ hours to show a movie 6 times with no time between showings. How long is the movie?

   The Action: _____Sharing equally_____

   The Operation: ___Division___ Answer: ___$1\frac{1}{4}$ hours___
   $(7\frac{1}{2} \div 6 = 1\frac{1}{4})$

3. There were 211 students and 20 adults on the trip. What was the total cost of admission for the students?

   The Action: _____Joining equal groups_____

   The Operation: ___Multiplication___ Answer: ___$263.75___
   $(211 \times 1.25 = 263.75)$

4. Posters at the museum cost $2.10 each. Paulo has $7.35. How many posters can he buy?

   The Action: _____Making groups of a given size_____

   The Operation: ___Division___ Answer: ___3 posters___
   $(7.35 \div 2.10 = 3.5;$ round down$)$

5. The museum has a special exhibit on the Ice Age. On Saturday, 937 people saw the exhibit. On Sunday, 895 people saw it. How many people saw the exhibit during the weekend?

   The Action: _____Joining different-sized groups_____

   The Operation: ___Addition___ Answer: ___1,832 people___
   $(937 + 895 = 1,832)$

Museum Admission	
Adults	$2.50
Students	$1.25
Children under 6	free

Additional word problems for Lesson 12 skills practice are on page 94.

Two-Operation Problems

What You Need to Know

Often, you will need to use two operations to solve a problem. Such a problem has a main question and a "hidden" question. Follow the same five problem solving steps, this time twice.

Step 1: As always, read the problem and reword the main question. Decide what the hidden question is.

Now follow Steps 2–5 to answer the hidden question.

Step 2: Find the needed facts.

Step 3: Plan what to do.

Step 4: Carry out the plan.

Step 5: Check the answer.

Once you answer the hidden question, repeat Steps 2–5 to answer the main question. Your answer to the hidden question is part of the data you need in Step 2.

Think About It

In a two-operation problem, why must you do all the steps twice?

Both the main and hidden questions must be solved (accurately).

Read each Example. The first operation is used for the hidden question. The second operation is used for the main question.

Example A Beth used 2 slices of whole wheat bread and 1 slice of roast chicken. How many calories are in the sandwich?

Hidden Question: *How many calories are in 2 slices of whole wheat bread?*

First Operation:	Second Operation:	Answer
Multiplication	*Addition*	to Main
55	110	**Question:**
× 2	+ 79	*189 calories*
110	189	

Example B Brian sliced 7 peaches to make dessert for 5 people. About how many calories were in each serving?

Hidden Question: *How many calories are in 7 peaches?*

First Operation:	Second Operation:	Answer
Multiplication	*Division*	**to Main**
35	49	**Question:**
× 7	5) 245	*about 49*
245		*calories*

Calorie Chart

Food	Calories
Apple, raw	117
Banana, fresh	119
Bread (1 slice)	
White	60
Whole Wheat	55
Butter (1 pat)	50
Cantaloupe (whole)	74
Cheese (1 slice)	
American	115
Swiss	105
Cheese (1 cup)	
Cottage	216
Chicken, roasted	
(1 slice)	79
Egg, boiled	77
Flounder (4 oz.)	78
Grapefruit	208
Milk (1 cup)	
Skim	87
Whole	165
Muffin, blueberry	125
Orange	106
Peach	35
Potato, baked	97
Strawberries, fresh	
(1 cup)	54
Turkey, roasted	
(1 slice)	100
Yogurt (1 cup)	
Skim milk	120

In Example A, you *multiply* to find the answer to the hidden question. Then you *add* that answer to the number of calories in 1 slice of chicken. This gives you the answer to the main question. In Example B, you *multiply* to find the answer to the hidden question. Then you *divide* that answer to find the answer to the main question.

Practice   Teacher Note: During discussion of the Practice items, have students state the "hidden" question in each.

For each problem, write the names of the two operations you will use. Then solve the problem. Be sure to follow the five steps to answer both the hidden and the main questions.

1. Susan usually drinks 5 cups of whole milk each day. How many fewer calories would she consume if she drank 5 cups of skim milk?

   First Operation: ____Subtraction____   Answer:

   Second Operation: ____Multiplication____   390 fewer calories

   (165 − 87 = 78; 5 × 78 = 390)

2. Ricky used 3 cups of strawberries, 4 oranges, and 5 apples to make a fruit salad. How many calories are in the fruit salad?

   First Operation: ____Multiplication____   Answer:

   Second Operation: ____Addition____   703 calories

   (3 × 54 = 162; 4 × 106 = 424; 5 × 117 = 585; 162 + 424 + 117 = 703)

3. Joanne ate a 455-calorie breakfast, a 379-calorie lunch, and a 726-calorie dinner. What was the *average* number of calories she consumed at each meal?

   First Operation: ____Addition____   Answer:

   Second Operation: ____Division____   520 calories

   (455 + 379 + 726 = 1,560; 1,560 ÷ 3 = 520)

4. Jeff used $\frac{1}{3}$ cup cottage cheese and $\frac{1}{2}$ cantaloupe to make an after-school snack. How many calories were in his snack?

   First Operation: ____Multiplication____   Answer:

   Second Operation: ____Addition____   109 calories

   ($\frac{1}{3}$ × 216 = 72; $\frac{1}{2}$ × 74 = 37; 72 + 37 = 109)

5. Lewis usually eats a banana and an apple with his lunch. Today he ate a peach and a grapefruit instead. How many more calories did he consume in today's fruit?

   First Operation: ____Addition____   Answer:

   Second Operation: ____Subtraction____   7 more calories

   (119 + 117 = 236; 35 + 208 = 243; 243 − 236 = 7)

Multiple-Step Problems

Aim: To solve problems that have more than one "hidden" question

What You Need to Know

Now you will solve problems with more than one "hidden" question. Thus, you will follow the five steps *more* than two times. These are **multiple-step problems.** You need to answer two or three hidden questions before you can answer the main question.

Think About It

In which step do you find the hidden questions? _Step 1_

Read each problem below. Notice the order in which the operations are used.

Example A Mandy is painting the 4 walls in her hobby shop. Each wall is 8.5 m long and 3.2 m high. A can of paint covers about 40 m². How many cans of paint does Mandy need to buy to give each wall one coat of paint?

Hidden Questions in Example A:
1. What is the area of one wall?
2. What is the total area of four walls?

First Operation: *Multiplication*
(Hidden Question 1)

$$\begin{array}{r} 3.2 \\ \times\ 8.5 \\ \hline 27.2 \end{array}$$

Second Operation: *Multiplication*
(Hidden Question 2)

$$\begin{array}{r} 27.2 \\ \times\ 4 \\ \hline 108.8 \end{array}$$

Third Operation: *Division*
(Main Question)

$$\begin{array}{r} 2.72 \\ 40\overline{)\,108.8} \end{array}$$

Answer to Main Question: *3 cans of paint*

Example B Mandy bought a computer for 15% off the list price. The list price was $695. Mandy made a $200 down payment. She agreed to pay the rest in 5 equal monthly payments. What were her monthly payments?

Hidden Questions in Example B:
1. How much did she save off the list price?
2. How much did she pay for the computer?
3. How much did she pay altogether in monthly payments?

First Operation: *Multiplication*
(Hidden Question 1)

$$\begin{array}{r} 695 \\ \times\ .15 \\ \hline 104.25 \end{array}$$

Second Operation: *Subtraction*
(Hidden Question 2)

$$\begin{array}{r} 695.00 \\ -\ 104.25 \\ \hline 590.75 \end{array}$$

Third Operation: *Subtraction*
(Hidden Question 3)

$$\begin{array}{r} 590.75 \\ -\ 200.00 \\ \hline 390.75 \end{array}$$

Fourth Operation: *Division*
(Main Question)

$$\begin{array}{r} 78.15 \\ 5\overline{)\,390.75} \end{array}$$

Answer to Main Question: *$78.15*

In Example A, there are two hidden questions and three operations. The first operation answers the first hidden question. The second operation answers the second one. The third operation answers the main question. In Example B, there are three hidden questions and four operations.

In Example A, Mandy cannot buy part of a can of paint. Interpret the remainder by rounding up to the next whole number.

Teacher Note: During discussion of the Practice items, have students state the "hidden" questions in each. Students may show some steps in a different order than shown below, depending on the order in which they are answering the hidden questions.

Practice

For each problem, write the order of operations you will use. Then solve the problem. Be sure to check *all* your answers.

1. Gary bought 3 model airplanes and 2 tubes of glue at the hobby shop. Each tube of glue cost $2.59. The total bill was $21.95. What was the average price Gary paid for the models?

First: __Multiplication (or addition)__   Second: __Subtraction__

Third: __Division__   Answer: __$5.59__
($2.59 × 2 = 5.18; 21.95 − 5.18 = 16.77; 16.77 ÷ 3 = 5.59$)

2. Tara bought a railroad car kit for $4.98 and some track for $6.42. The sales clerk added 5% sales tax to the cost of her purchases. What was her total bill? (Remember: 5% = 0.05.)

First: __Addition__   Second: __Multiplication__

Third: __Addition__   Answer: __$11.97__
($4.98 + 6.42 = 11.40; 11.40 × .05 = .57; 11.40 + .57 = 11.97$)

3. Marcos works at the hobby shop. He earns $5.40 per hour for the first 35 hours he works. He earns $8.10 for each hour beyond that. One week, he worked $43\frac{1}{2}$ hours. What did he earn?

First: __Subtraction__   Second: __Multiplication__

Third: __Multiplication__   Fourth: __Addition__

Answer: __$257.85__
($43\frac{1}{2} − 35 = 8\frac{1}{2}; 35 × 5.40 = 189; 8\frac{1}{2} × 8.10 = 68.85; 189 + 68.85 = 257.85$)

4. The hobby shop had a special 25% off sale on all kites. Maria bought 3 box kites and 1 tetra kite during the sale. How much did the kites cost before sales tax was added?

First: __Multiplication__   Second: __Addition__

Third: __Multiplication__   Fourth: __Subtraction__

Answer: __$13.35__
($3.95 × 3 = 11.85; 11.85 + 5.95 = 17.80; 17.80 × .25 = 4.45; 17.80 − 4.45 = 13.35$)

Kites	
	Reg. Price
Box Style	$3.95
Tetra Style	$5.95
All Others	$2.95

SPECIAL: 25% off regular price!

Additional word problems for Lesson 14 skills practice are on page 96.

Checking Estimates and Computations

Aim: To use estimation and computation checks to judge whether an answer is reasonable and accurate

What You Need to Know

You check an answer to see if it is (1) reasonable and (2) accurate. To check your computations, do one of the following:

- Add or multiply "backwards" (switch the numbers).
- Subtract to check addition; add to check subtraction.
- Divide to check multiplication; multiply to check division.

What if a computation checks as accurate but the answer makes no sense? You may have labeled your answer with the wrong unit. Or, you may have used the wrong plan.

Think About It

How can an answer be wrong if the computation is accurate?

The wrong unit or a wrong plan may have been used.

Read the Examples. Notice how the computations are checked.

Example A Rudy, Tom, and Bev ran for class president. Rudy got 135 votes; Tom got 171 votes; Bev got 212 votes. How many votes were cast in the election?

Estimation:	100	**Computation:**	135
	200		171
	+ 200		+ 212
	500		518

Estimated Answer: *500 votes*

Computed Answer: *518 votes*

Computation Check: *212 + 171 + 135 = 518*

Example B Bev's friends worked from 3:10 P.M. until 6:05 P.M. making election posters. How long did they work?

Estimation:	6	**Computation:**	6 hr. 5 min.
	− 3		− 3 hr. 10 min.
	3		2 hr. 55 min.

Estimated Answer: *3 hours*

Computed Answer: 2 hr. 55 min.

Computation Check: 2 hr. 55 min.
                     + 3 hr. 10 min.
                     5 hr. 65 min., or 6 hr. 5 min.

In Example A, you *multiply* to find the answer to the hidden question. Then you *add* that answer to the number of calories in 1 slice of chicken. This gives you the answer to the main question. In Example B, you *multiply* to find the answer to the hidden question. Then you *divide* that answer to find the answer to the main question.

Practice

Follow all five steps to solve each word problem below. Then write the estimated answer and the computed answer. Show your computation check in the box next to each word problem.

Teacher Note: Students' computation checks may vary from the examples given in the boxes.

Morris School Enrollment	
6th Graders	547
7th Graders	582
8th Graders	683

1. If 518 eighth-graders voted in the class election, how many eighth-graders did not vote?

   Estimated Answer: ___200 eighth-___graders
   (700 − 500 = 200)

   Computed Answer: ___165 eighth-___graders
   (683 − 518 = 165)

   1. Computation Check

   $$\begin{array}{r} 165 \\ + 518 \\ \hline 683 \end{array}$$

2. The seventh-grade class elections will be held next week. If $\frac{5}{6}$ of the seventh-graders vote in the election, how many seventh-graders will vote?

   Estimated Answer: ___500 seventh-___graders
   (600 ÷ 6 = 100; 100 × 5 = 500)

   Computed Answer: ___485 seventh-___graders
   ($\frac{5}{6}$ × 582 = 485)

   2. Computation Check

   $$\begin{array}{r} 582 \\ \times \frac{5}{6} \\ \hline 485 \end{array}$$

3. Rudy's friends made 23 election posters. They hung the same number of posters in 6 different classrooms. The extra posters were hung in the library. How many posters did they hang in each classroom?

   Estimated Answer: ___4 posters___
   (24 ÷ 6 = 4)

   Computed Answer: ___3 posters___
   (23 ÷ 6 = $3\frac{5}{6}$, round down)

   3. Computation Check

   $$\begin{array}{r} 3\frac{5}{6} \\ \times 6 \\ \hline 23 \end{array}$$

4. Juan, Claire, and Sue ran for eighth-grade class secretary. Juan received 186 votes. Claire and Sue each received the same number of votes as each other. If 518 students voted for class secretary, how many votes did Claire receive?

   Estimated Answer: ___150 votes___
   (500 − 200 = 300; 300 ÷ 2 = 150)

   Computed Answer: ___166 votes___
   (518 − 186 = 332; 332 ÷ 2 = 166)

   4. Computation Check

   $$\begin{array}{rr} 332 & 166 \\ + 186 & \times 2 \\ \hline 518 & 332 \end{array}$$

5. The new class officers are planning a party for the whole school. They expect that $\frac{2}{3}$ of the students will attend the party. How many students do they expect to attend the party?

   Estimated Answer: ___1,200___students
   (500 + 600 + 700 = 1,800)

   Computed Answer: ___1,208___students
   (547 + 582 + 683 = 1,182; 1,182 × $\frac{2}{3}$ = 1,208)

   5. Computation Check

   $$\begin{array}{rr} 683 & \text{or} \quad \frac{2}{3} \\ 582 & \times 1,812 \\ + 547 & \overline{1,208} \\ \hline 1,812 & \end{array}$$

Additional word problems for Lesson 15 skills practice are on page 97.

Unit 2 Review

A. On each line, write **T** or **F** to tell whether the statement is true or false.

__F__   1. Problems in daily life always have just the right amount of information.

__T__   2. When you need to find facts on a map, it is important first to study the whole map.

__T__   3. A table helps to organize all the numbers on a bus, train, or airline schedule.

__T__   4. You should read the title and all the labels on a graph before you begin to look for a specific fact.

__F__   5. Facts needed to solve a problem are always found somewhere on the problem page.

__T__   6. Routine word problems can be solved by adding, subtracting, multiplying, or dividing.

__F__   7. To join equal groups to find a total, the correct operation is subtraction.

__T__   8. When solving two-operation problems, you follow the same five steps— but you follow them twice.

__T__   9. Multiple-step problems may have two or more "hidden" questions to answer.

__F__   10. When checking your answer, if your computation is accurate, then your answer must be correct.

B. On each line, write the word that best completes the sentence.

__facts__   11. To solve a word problem, you must have all the needed _____.

__line__   12. A type of graph that can be used to show change over time is a _____ graph.

__operation__   13. To choose the correct _____ in a routine problem, visualize the action.

__main__   14. The answer to a hidden question becomes a fact needed for answering the _____ question.

__backward__   15. To check addition or multiplication computations, you can add or multiply _____ (switch the numbers).

C. Circle the letter of the correct answer.

16. After dinner, Kris spent $\frac{1}{2}$ hour doing his math homework, $1\frac{1}{2}$ hours watching TV, and $1\frac{1}{4}$ hours doing his science homework. How much time did he spend doing homework?

    a. $1\frac{3}{4}$ hours　　**b.** $3\frac{1}{4}$ hours　　**c.** 2 hours　　**d.** $1\frac{2}{6}$ hours

17. Doug drove from Hartford through Norwich and New London to Newport. How many miles did he drive?

    a. 116 miles　　**c.** 102 miles

    b. 92 miles　　**d.** 114 miles

Driving Distances between Connecticut and Rhode Island

(All distances in miles.)

18. Sue took the 8:05 P.M. train from Boswell to Woodland Station. How long was her train ride?

    a. 58 min.　　　**c.** 1 hr. 3 min.

    b. 48 min.　　　**d.** 52 min.

Train Schedule

	Departs		Arrives Woodland Station
Tyler	Boswell	Spring	
6:10 A.M.	6:25 A.M.	6:35 A.M.	7:07 A.M.
8:30 A.M.	8:45 A.M.	8:55 A.M.	9:27 A.M.
5:25 P.M.	5:40 P.M.	5:50 P.M.	6:22 P.M.
7:50 P.M.	8:05 P.M.	8:35 P.M.	8:53 P.M.

19. How many more students were absent on Thursday than on Tuesday?

    a. 13 students　　**c.** 14 students

    b. 12 students　　**d.** 15 students

20. A large paper clip has a mass of 4 grams. A box of these clips has a mass of 1 kilogram. How many clips are in the box?

    a. 25 clips　　　**c.** 4,000 clips

    b. 4 clips　　　**d.** 250 clips

21. There are 23 rows of seats in the theater. Each row has 38 seats. How many people can be seated in the theater?

    a. 61 people　　**c.** 854 people

    b. 874 people　　**d.** 774 people

Students Absent

22. A slice of whole wheat bread has 55 calories. A slice of roast turkey has 100 calories. Adam used two slices of whole wheat bread and 1 slice of turkey to make a sandwich. How many calories were in his sandwich?

    a. 310 calories　　**b.** 155 calories　　**c.** 210 calories　　**d.** 255 calories

23. Sheri bought 4 markers and 3 notebooks. Her total bill was $6.35. Each notebook cost $1.25. What was the price of each marker?

    a. $1.28　　**b.** $0.65　　**c.** $2.60　　**d.** $0.85

D. Read and reread each word problem. Then follow the directions to show your solution to the problem.

5 centimeters
4 centimeters
9 centimeters

24. Find the area of the triangle shown.
   a. Underline the question.
   b. Circle the needed facts in the problem.

   c. Describe your plan: ___Use a formula: A = ½bh.___

   _____

   d. If an estimate can be made, show it here: ___½ × 36 = 18___

   e. Carry out your plan. Answer: ___18 square centimeters (½ × 4 × 9 = 18)___

   f. Check your answer. If you got an incorrect answer, tell how you know it is wrong. Then write the correct answer.

   ___Students who got incorrect answers should mention computation error or___

   ___that the answer was not reasonable.___

25. Megan had 43 photos of the class party and 21 photos of the class field trip. Suppose she puts 4 pictures on each page in her photo album. How many pages does she use?
   a. Underline the question.
   b. Circle the needed facts in the problem.

   c. Describe your plan: ___Add and divide (number of photos of class party +___

   ___number of photos of field trip = total photos; total photos ÷ number per___

   ___page = number of pages)___
   d. If an estimate can be made, show it here: ___(40 + 20) ÷ 4 = 15___

   e. Carry out your plan. Answer: ___16 pages   ([43 + 21] ÷ 4 = 16)___

   f. Check your answer. If you got an incorrect answer, tell how you know it is wrong. Then write the correct answer.

   ___Students who got incorrect answers should mention computation error or___

   ___that the answer was not reasonable.___

3 More Help With Strategies

- Making a Diagram ▪ Making a Line Graph ▪ Writing an Equation ▪ Using a Formula ▪ Solving a Simpler Problem ▪ Using Ratio Proportions ▪ Using Logical Reasoning ▪ Exact or Estimated Answers ▪ More Than One Strategy

Making a Diagram

What You Need to Know

If you have a problem you are not sure how to solve, begin by making a diagram of it. Then reread the problem. Ask yourself, "Is my drawing accurate? Have I included all the facts I can?" Then use the diagram and any other facts in the problem to decide on your plan for solving the problem.

Think About It

Why does it help to draw a diagram of a problem?

The diagram helps you to "see" the action in the problem.

Read each problem below. Notice how each diagram helps.

Example A Julie watched a worker ant in an ant farm. The ant started at the surface. It dug straight down 1.5 cm and went back up. Then it went straight down the same tunnel for 3 cm and returned to the surface. On the third trip, it went straight down 4.5 cm and rested. How far did the ant travel in all?

Make a Diagram: **Answer:** *13.5 cm*

Example B The ant farm is 40 cm wide and 30 cm high. One worker ant walked all around the outside edge of the farm. It stopped to rest every 10 cm. How many times did the ant stop to rest during its trip around the farm?

Make a Diagram: **Answer:** *14 times*

In Example A, notice the arrows in the diagram. They show the distances and the directions the ant walked. Add 1.5 + 1.5 + 3 + 3 + 4.5. Example B shows each point around the farm where the ant stopped to rest. Count the points.

Practice

For each problem, make a diagram in the space provided. Write the answer. (Remember to check your answer for sense.)

1. At the science fair, all the electricity experiments are placed on one large square table. To make the large table, 9 smaller tables were pushed together. Each small square table is $1\frac{1}{2}$ yards on a side. What is the perimeter of the larger square? (Hint: *Perimeter* means "distance around.")

   Answer: ___18 yards___

   1. Diagram

   1½ yd. 1½ yd. 1½ yd.

   4 × 4½ = 18

2. Glenn has six different-colored dyes. The colors are red, blue, yellow, green, orange, and purple. He wants to mix 1 cup of each dye with 1 cup of every other dye to form new colors. How many new colors will he make?

   Answer: ___15 new colors___

   Teacher Note: Students should count while drawing the connecting lines. You may want to point out that this type of problem may also be solved by doing an organized list.

   2. Diagram

   blue   yellow

   red   green

   purple   orange

3. Beth is experimenting with solutions in test tubes. In each test tube, she places either water or alcohol. To each liquid, she adds salt or sugar. She then heats or cools each mixture. How many test tubes does Beth need to test all possible combinations? (Hint: Remember the branching "tree diagram" from Book 1.)

   Answer: ___8 test tubes___

   3. Diagram

   water — salt — heat / cool — sugar — heat / cool
   alcohol — salt — heat / cool — sugar — heat / cool

4. Write a word problem of your own. Write a problem that making a diagram would help you to solve.

   Answers will vary, but check that making a diagram would indeed

   help to solve the problem. This is a good Practice item around which

   to hold class discussion.

Teacher Note: Many of the lessons in Unit 3 end with a Practice item that has students write their own word problems. This item will help students to understand the types of problems that can be solved using the strategy learned in each lesson.

Making a Line Graph

Aim: To solve problems that involve constant speed or rate of change by making line graphs

What You Need to Know

A **line graph** is a special type of diagram. It helps you to "see" the data in a problem. Use a line graph in order to—

- **find unknown values that fall "in between" known values.** Suppose a car is traveling at a constant speed of 37 miles per hour. A line graph of this will tell you *how far* the car will travel in *any* amount of time.
- **compare similar events.** Suppose a fast-moving train starts traveling 1 minute after a slow-moving train. When will the faster train overtake the slower train? Make line graphs for both trains on the same grid. The trains will meet where the two lines cross.

> **To solve a problem by making a graph:**
> 1) Make a table.
> 2) Put the data from the problem in the table.
> 3) Find the pattern in the data.
> 4) Extend the table to 3 pairs of numbers.
> 5) Make the graph using the extended data.

Think About It

In the Example, what are the labels in the table and the graph?

They are the same: Time (number of hours), Distance (in miles).

Study the Example. Notice how the table and graph are used.

Example A car moving at a constant speed travels 75 miles in 2 hours. How far will the car travel in 6 hours?

Make a table (label, extend):

Time (number of hours)	1	2	3
Distance (in miles)	37.5	75	112.5

Make a graph (label, plot points, draw line):

Answer (read the graph): *225 miles*

In the Example, you "read up" from 6 hours to where the grid line crosses the graphed line. Then "read left" to find that the car has traveled 225 miles. Suppose you wanted to find out how long it would take the car to travel 300 miles. How would you read the graph?

Practice

Teacher Note: To answer the above question, you would "read right" from 300 miles and then "read down" to 8 hours.

Teacher Note: Students may choose a different series of three points to plot in Practice items 1 and 3, but their graphed lines should look the same. Also, students may choose to label the x- and y-axes opposite to the way they are shown in item 3.

For each problem, first make a table with three pairs of numbers. Then make a graph by plotting points and drawing a line.

1. Maria is saving to buy a $180 typewriter. She saves the same amount each week. After 3 weeks she has saved $60. How long will it take her to save enough to buy the typewriter?

Make a table:

Time (number of weeks)	1	2	3
Money (in dollars)	20	40	60

Make a graph: Answer: _____9 weeks_____

2. How much money will Maria have saved in 7 weeks? _____$140_____

3. Ron started working at 9 A.M. and makes $6 per hour. Jay started working at 10 A.M. and makes $8 per hour. At what time will they both have made the same amount of money?

Table for Ron:

Time	9 A.M.	10 A.M.	11 A.M.
Amount Earned	0	6	12

Table for Jay:

Time	10 A.M.	11 A.M.	12 A.M.
Amount Earned	0	8	16

Make a graph for both boys on the same grid: Answer: _____1 P.M._____

4. How much will each boy earn by noon? _____Ron: $18; Jay: $16_____

Additional word problems for Lesson 17 skills practice are on page 99.

Writing an Equation

Aim: To solve problems by writing equations using one or more of the four operations

What You Need to Know

You can use equations to solve many word problems. Numbers, letters, and symbols stand for information in the problems. A letter, called a **variable**, stands for an unknown number.

You need to think about the "actions" in problems. This will help you decide which operations to use. Remember:

- **Add** to join different-sized groups.
- **Multiply** to join same-sized groups.
- **Subtract** to find how many are left or to compare amounts.
- **Divide** to break a group down into smaller, equal groups.

Often, more than one equation can be used. For instance, each of these could be used to describe the same situation:

$$n + 3 = 7 \qquad 3 + n = 7 \qquad 7 - n = 3 \qquad 7 - 3 = n$$

Think About It

Why should you think about the action in a problem?

The action will help you decide which operation to use.

Read each problem. Notice how the variable is described. The equation is written *after* you think about the problem in phrases.

Example A Marty spent 15 hours building a patio for the Lovells. He charged them $1,200 for the patio. The materials cost $897.25. What was Marty's profit?

Variable: *Let n = Marty's profit*

Think: *price charged − cost of materials = profit*

Equation: *1,200 − 897.25 = n*   **Answer:** *$302.75*

Example B Mrs. Lovell budgeted $45 to buy bushes to go around her patio. Bushes are on sale for $5.75. How many can Mrs. Lovell buy and still stay within budget?

Variable: *Let n = number of bushes budgeted for*

Think: *money budgeted ÷ price per bush = bushes budgeted for*

Equation: *45.00 ÷ 5.75 = n*

Answer: *7 bushes (budgeted for 7.83 bushes)*

In Example A, the action could suggest either subtraction or addition. A subtraction equation is used. You could also use the addition equation 897.25 + n = 1,200 (cost of materials + profit = amount charged). In Example B, the answer to the equation is not the final answer. Reread the question! The number of bushes Mrs. Lovell can *buy* is 7.

Teacher Note: Often, different equations can be written to solve the same problem. Still, you may want to point out that as students carry out the plan for solving an equation, the aim is to get the variable (*n*) alone on one side of the equal sign. Then the operation that will actually be computed is on the other side.

Practice

For each problem, describe the variable. Think about the action in the problem. Then write the equation and the answer. (Don't forget to follow all five problem solving steps!)

1. Mrs. Lovell drew this diagram of her new patio. What is the perimeter of the patio? (Do you need to look up *perimeter* in the Appendix?)

   Variable: Let P = _____the perimeter_____

   Equation: ___$P = (2 \times 12\frac{1}{2}) + (2 \times 9\frac{3}{4})$___ Answer: ___$44\frac{1}{2}$ feet___

$9\frac{3}{4}$ ft.

$12\frac{1}{2}$ ft.

2. Marty put new baseboard molding in 2 bedrooms. He used 63 feet of molding for 1 bedroom. This is $1\frac{1}{2}$ times as much molding as he used in the second bedroom. How much molding did he use in the second bedroom?

   Variable: Let n = ___amount of molding used in second bedroom___

   Equation: ___$1\frac{1}{2} \times n = 63$___ Answer: ___42 feet___

3. Marty is replacing 4 windows with screens in the Snyder house. Each window costs $59. Each screen is an additional $4.95. How much will it cost for the 4 new windows and screens?

   Variable: Let n = ___total cost of new windows and screens___

   Equation: ___$4(59 + 4.95) = n$___ Answer: ___$255.80___

4. Jill drew this diagram of her backyard. Marty is putting in a new fence along the back and one side. Fencing comes in 6-foot sections. How many sections of fencing should Marty buy?

   Variable: Let n = ___number of fence sections he needs___

   Equation: ___$(47 + 22.5) \div 6 = n$___ Answer: ___12 sections___
   (needs 11.58 sections)

5. Write a word problem of your own. Write a problem that can be solved with an equation.

   ___Answers will vary, but check that the problem can be solved by writing___

   ___an equation. This would be a good item for class discussion.___

Jill's house

47 ft.

22.5 ft.

Additional word problems for Lesson 18 skills practice are on page 100.

45

Using a Formula

Aim: To solve problems using rate formulas

What You Need to Know

Teacher Note: You may wish to review with students the structure of formulas (e.g., known vs. unknown variables) using the geometric formulas on Appendix page 121 as examples. These were learned in Book 1 and are more tangible than the rate formulas taught in this lesson.

A **formula** is a special kind of equation. It is useful for solving certain types of problems. These are problems that have the same basic situation. The numbers are all that change. Review some common formulas on Appendix page 121.

In this lesson, you will use two formulas that contain the variable r to stand for "rate." The word *rate* means a measured change. It is "something per something," as in miles per hour or percent per year.

$d = rt$ (distance = rate × time)

$i = prt$ (interest = principal × rate × time)

The formula $d = rt$ solves certain kinds of **motion** problems. The distance, the rate, *or* the time is unknown. The formula $i = prt$ is used to compute **simple interest**. In a word problem for this formula, *one* of the following is unknown:

- Interest (i) is the amount paid for the use of money.
- Principal (p) is the amount borrowed or invested.
- Rate (r) is the percent at which interest is charged or earned per year.
- Time (t) is the number of years for which the money is borrowed or invested.

Of course, we expect you to pay us money for this!

Think About It

What words do the letters in the interest formula ($i = prt$) stand for?

interest	=	principal	×	rate	×	time

Read each problem. Notice how letters are replaced by numbers.

Example A A runner ran a distance of 26 miles in $2\frac{1}{2}$ hours. What was the runner's average rate of speed?

The Formula: $d = rt$

Replace the letters you know: $26 = r × 2\frac{1}{2}$

Answer: *10.4 miles per hour*

Example B Irene borrowed $1,800 at an interest rate of 9.5% for 6 months. How much interest did she pay on her loan?

The Formula: $i = prt$

Replace the letters you know: $i = 1,800 × .095 × .5$

Answer: *$85.50*

In Example A, the formula $d = rt$ is used to find the runner's average rate of speed. The distance is in miles and the time is in hours. So, the rate is shown as miles per hour.

In Example B, the formula $i = prt$ is used. Notice that the percent is written as a decimal ($9.5\% = 0.095$). The time is in years (6 months = 0.5 year). When you use this formula, always change the percent to a decimal. Always show the time in years.

Practice

Teacher Note: During discussion of the Practice items, focus students' attention on whether their answers make sense. Are students remembering to check for this as part of Step 5?

Use the formula $d = rt$ or $i = prt$ to solve each problem.

1. A car is moving at a rate of 50 miles per hour. How long will it take the car to travel 625 miles?

   The formula: __$d = rt$__   Replace letters: __$625 = 50 \times t$__

   Answer: __12½ hours__

2. Casey invested $1,000 at 5% simple interest for $3\frac{1}{2}$ years. How much interest did he earn?

   The formula: __$i = prt$__   Replace letters: __$i = 1,000 \times .05 \times 3.5$__

   Answer: __$175__

3. An airplane travels a distance of 3,025 miles in 5 hours 30 minutes. At what rate of speed is the airplane traveling?

   The formula: __$d = rt$__   Replace letters: __$3,025 = r \times 5\frac{1}{2}$__

   Answer: __550 miles per hour__

4. Rosita invested $850 for 2 years at simple interest. After 2 years, she had earned $119. What was the interest rate?

   The formula: __$i = prt$__   Replace letters: __$119 = 850 \times r \times 2$__

   Answer: __7%__

5. Jake borrowed $1,500 at 12.5% interest. For how long did he borrow the money if the interest he paid was $562.50?

   The formula: __$i = prt$__   Replace letters: __$562.50 = 1,500 \times .125 \times t$__

   Answer: __3 years__

6. Write a word problem of your own. Write a problem that you could use one of the rate formulas to solve.

   __Answers will vary, but check that using one of the rate formulas__

   __will help to solve the problem. This would be a good item for class__

   __discussion.__

Solving a Simpler Problem

What You Need to Know

A problem with hard numbers or with a complex situation can seem harder than it really is. Leave it for a moment. Think of a similar but simpler problem. How would you solve it? Then apply the same plan to the original problem. Sometimes, you will need to solve several simpler problems in order to find a *pattern* in how the answers are found. You will learn more about that in this lesson.

Think About It

What can make word problems seem hard to solve?

Difficult numbers or situations can make problems seem hard.

Read each problem. Notice how the situation is made simpler.

Example A How many triangles are in this figure?

Simplify: *Look at the figure in stages starting from the inside and working out.*

1st stage ▼ 1 triangle

2nd stage 3 small + 1 larger = 4 triangles

3rd stage ▽ 3 small + 1 larger = 4 triangles

Pattern: *Each stage after the first adds 4 new triangles.*
Answer: *21 triangles (1 + 4 + 4 + 4 + 4 + 4 = 21)*

Example B There are 18 members in the chess club. If each mem-ber plays one chess game with every other member, how many chess games will be played?

Simplify: *Think about the number of games if there were 2, 3, or 4 members in the club.*

Pattern: *The number of games is the sum of the numbers from 1-less-than-the-number-of-members down to 1.*
Answer: *153 chess games (17 + 16 + 15 + ... + 1)*

In Example A, simplify the problem by looking at each stage of the figure. The first, innermost piece is one small triangle. Each stage after that adds 4 new triangles. There are five 4-triangle stages. There are, therefore, 21 triangles in all.

Example B is simplified by thinking about a club with 2, 3, or 4 members. That establishes the pattern for finding the number of games for any number of members. Then apply that pattern to 18 members.

Practice

For each problem, think of similar but simpler problems. Explain the pattern. Then use it to solve the original problem.

1. How many triangles are in this figure?

   Pattern: _Each stage has 4 triangles; multiply the number of stages_

   _by 4._

   _____ Answer: _32 triangles_

   _(8 × 4 = 32)_

2. There are 15 students who have signed up to play in the annual handball tournament. If each student plays every other student, how many games will be played? (Hint: Look again at Example B.)

   Pattern: _Add the numbers from 1-less-than-the-number-of-students_

   down to 1.

   _____ Answer: _105 games_

   _(14 + 13 + 12 + ... + 1 = 105)_

	Tables	People
	1	4
	2	6
	3	8
	4	9

3. Terri has 15 small, square tables. She plans to use the tables for a party. Each table can seat one person on a side. If all the tables are pushed together to make one long table, how many people can sit at that table?

   Pattern: _Multiply the number of tables by 2 and then add 2._

   _____ Answer: _32 people_

   _([15 × 2] + 2 = 32)_

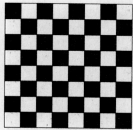

4. How many squares are in a checkerboard? The squares can be different sizes and they can overlap. (Hint: Think about the number of squares in a 1 × 1 square, a 2 × 2 square, and a 3 × 3 square.)

   Pattern: _Add the numbers that would be the areas of each size of_

   square up to 8 × 8.

   _____ Answer: _204 squares_

   _(1 + 4 + 9 + 16 + ... + 64 = 204)_

Additional word problems for Lesson 20 skills practice are on page 102.

Using Ratio Proportions

What You Need to Know

A **ratio** is a way to compare numbers. A ratio can be shown as a fraction. Suppose that you drink 3 cups of milk with every 2 muffins you eat. The ratio of cups of milk to muffins is 3 to 2. Shown as a fraction, this ratio is $\frac{3}{2}$. Ratios can be used to solve problems that involve rates or comparisons.

A **proportion** is an equation that states that two ratios are equal. A proportion is true if the *cross products* are equal.

Cross Products
$2 \times 6 = 12$
$3 \times 4 = 12$

Therefore, $\frac{3}{2} = \frac{6}{4}$ is a proportion.

If you know any three numbers in a proportion, you can find the fourth number. Use cross products to write an equation.

Think About It

A proportion is an _____equation_____ stating that two

_____ratios_____ are equal.

Read each problem. Notice how the proportion is set up and solved in each.

Example A Sean's recipe for waffles calls for 1.5 cups of flour for every 2 eggs. If Sean uses 6 cups of flour, how many eggs should he use?

The Proportion: $\frac{1.5}{2} \times \frac{6}{n}$ $\dfrac{\text{cups of flour}}{\text{number of eggs}}$

The Cross Products: $1.5n = 12; n = 12 \div 1.5; n = 8$
Answer: *8 eggs*

Example B This is a scale drawing of Beth's apartment. The scale is written below the drawing. Use the drawing and the scale to find the real width of Beth's kitchen. (Hint: First measure the width of the kitchen on the scale drawing.)

The Proportion: $\frac{2}{3} \times \frac{2}{n}$ $\dfrac{\text{length on drawing (in cm)}}{\text{actual length (in m)}}$

The Cross Products: $2n = 6; n = 3$
Answer: *3 meters*

Bedroom | Bedroom

Bath

Living Room | Kitchen

Dining Area

Scale: 2 cm = 3 m

In Example A, read the proportion as "1.5 cups of flour is to 2 eggs as 6 cups of flour is to *n* eggs." Use the cross products to write an equation to solve for the unknown (*n* eggs). Example B shows how to use equal ratios to solve problems involving scale drawings.

Practice

For each problem, write the proportion in the box. Then write the cross products and the answer. Use the scale drawing on page 50 for items 1 and 2.

1. What is the actual length of Beth's living room?

   Cross Products: _____ $2n = 12; n = 6$ _____   Answer: _____ 6 meters _____

   1. The Proportion

   $$\frac{2}{3} = \frac{4}{n}$$

2. Beth wants to add onto her house a garage that is 7.5 meters wide. She will use the same scale as was used for her house. How wide will the garage be in her scale drawing?

   Cross Products: _____ $3n = 15; n = 5$ _____   Answer: _____ 5 centimeters _____

   2. The Proportion

   $$\frac{2}{3} = \frac{n}{7.5}$$

3. Alex is making spaghetti sauce for a school fund-raising dinner. He needs 2 cups of sauce for every 5 people. He wants to make enough sauce for 240 people. How many *gallons* of sauce should he make? (Hint: First find how many cups of sauce he needs. Then convert cups to gallons.)

   Cross Products: _____ $5n = 480; n = 96$ _____   Answer: _____ 6 gallons _____ (96 cups; 96 ÷ 16 = 6)

   3. The Proportion

   $$\frac{2}{5} = \frac{n}{240}$$

4. Alex's recipe calls for 5 onions for every 3 pounds of meat. If he uses 42 pounds of meat, how many onions will he need?

   Cross Products: _____ $3n = 210; n = 70$ _____   Answer: _____ 70 onions _____

   4. The Proportion

   $$\frac{5}{3} = \frac{n}{42}$$

5. Lucia drives 140 miles in 3.5 hours. At this rate, how far will she drive in 6.5 hours?

   Cross Products: _____ $3.5n = 910; n = 260$ _____   Answer: _____ 260 miles _____

   5. The Proportion

   $$\frac{140}{3.5} = \frac{n}{6.5}$$

6. Write a word problem of your own. Write a problem that using a proportion (equal ratios) would help to solve.

   Answers will vary, but check that using a proportion will help to solve

   the problem. This would be a good item for class discussion.

Using Logical Reasoning

Aim: To solve problems by using deductive logic

What You Need to Know

Logical reasoning is a way to solve "puzzle" problems. Puzzle problems have many *possible* answers. There are clues in the problems. You need to use logical reasoning, or **deductive logic,** as you read the clues. Then you can rule out or approve each possible answer.

A table or chart can be used to organize the facts in a puzzle problem. As you read the clues, mark the outcomes in the table. These problems will differ from others you have done. They often do not include numbers.

Think About It

Why is a table helpful when you use logic to solve a problem?

A table helps to organize the facts.

Read the Example. Notice how the table is set up and marked.

Example   Ann, Barb, and Sara each get to school a different way. One rides a bus, one roller-skates, and one walks. Use the clues to find out how each girl gets to school.

Clue 1: Barb and the walker eat lunch together.

Clue 2: The bus rider swims on Ann's team.

Clue 3: Sara roller-skates to school.

Set Up a Table: Mark the table for each clue. Use X to rule out a choice. Use ✔ to approve a choice.

After Clue 1: You know Barb is NOT the walker. Place an X in Barb's column across from "Walk."

After Clue 2: You know Ann is NOT the bus rider. Put an X in Ann's column across from "Bus."

After Clue 3: You know Sara is the roller skater. Put a ✔ in Sara's column across from "Skates."

Solve the Puzzle: From what you have marked on the table, you can solve the puzzle.

- Since Sara is the roller skater, she cannot be the walker or the bus rider. Put X's there.

- There is only one choice left for the bus rider — Barb. Complete her column.

- Ann must be the walker!

After Clue 2

	Ann	Barb	Sara
Bus	X	✔	X
Skates	X	X	✔
Walk	✔	X	X

After Clue 1 —   After Clue 3

In the Example, the clues are considered one at a time. The table is marked with an X (to rule out a possible solution) or with a ✓ (to approve a possible solution). After all the clues are marked, the table is studied to solve the puzzle.

Practice

For each item 1–4, first set up a table on a separate sheet of paper. Mark your table for each clue. After you solve the problem, be sure to check your answer against the clues. Then write your answer here.

1. Dan, Lisa, and Amy have different occupations. They work as an accountant, a baker, and a carpenter. Use the clues to find each person's occupation.
   Clue 1: Dan and the accountant play tennis together.
   Clue 2: The carpenter helped Amy build a garage.
   Clue 3: Lisa's bakery shop is open six days a week.

   Answer: ___Dan is a carpenter, Lisa is a baker, and Amy is an accountant.___

	Dan	Lisa	Amy
Accountant	X	X	✓
Baker	X	✓	X
Carpenter	✓	X	X

2. Ray, Sue, and Carlos each read a book about their favorite sport. The books were about swimming, soccer, and tennis. Use the clues to find what Carlos's book was about.
   Clue 1: One of Sue's friends likes swimming.
   Clue 2: Ray likes to swim.
   Clue 3: The one who likes tennis asked Carlos to play a game.

   Answer: ___Carlos's book is soccer.___

	Ray	Sue	Carlos
Swimming	✓	X	X
Soccer	X	X	✓
Tennis	X	✓	X

3. Fawn, Fern, and Felix are movie-goers. One likes monster movies, one likes romantic movies, and one likes space movies. The one who likes monster movies lives next door to Fern. The ones who like romantic and monster movies helped Felix to find his lost homework. Who likes which kind of movies?

   Answer: ___Fawn likes monster movies, Fern likes romantic movies, and Felix likes space movies.___

	Fawn	Fern	Felix
Monster	✓	X	X
Romantic	X	✓	X
Space	X	X	✓

4. Jason, Jacob, Joel, and James each own a different pet. They have a dog, a cat, a hamster, and a rabbit. Jason has the smallest pet. The dog and cat owners both took care of Joel's pet when he went on vacation. Jacob's dog likes to chase the cat up a tree. What kind of pet does James own?

   Answer: ___James owns a cat.___

	Jason	Jacob	Joel	James
Dog	X	✓	X	X
Cat	X	X	X	✓
Hamster	✓	X	X	X
Rabbit	X	X	✓	X

5. Write a word problem of your own. Write a problem that using logical reasoning would help you to solve.

   Answers will vary, but check that using deductive logic would help to

   solve the problem. This would be a good item for class discussion.

Exact or Estimated Answers

Aim: To decide which problems can be solved by finding estimated rather than exact answers

What You Need to Know

You use estimated numbers as often as exact numbers in your daily life. You estimate when an exact answer is *not possible*. (How many people will be born in the U.S. next year? How many fish are in a lake?) You also estimate when an exact number is *not needed*. (About how much time do you spend studying each week? Do you have enough money to buy a taco for lunch?)

Before you decide on a plan for solving a word problem, ask yourself, "Do I need an exact answer? Or, is an estimated answer enough?" If an estimated answer is enough, you may be able to do the work mentally.

Think About It

When can you use an estimated answer to solve a problem?

Do this when an exact answer is not possible or not needed.

Read each problem. Notice whether an exact or estimated answer is used to solve the problem.

Example A Yoko has saved $40 to buy new school clothes. She wants to buy a skirt for $18.95, a sweater for $11.25, and a belt for $3.95. Does she have enough money?

Exact or Estimated? *Estimated*

The Execution: *Think: 20 + 10 + 4 = 34*

The Answer: *Yes, Yoko has enough money.*

Example B The tax on the three items Yoko bought in Example A was $1.71. Yoko wants to pay for these 3 items by check. For how much should she write the check?

Exact or Estimated? *Exact*

The Execution:
```
 18.95
 11.25
  3.95
  1.71
 35.86
```

Answer: *$35.86*

How many potholes are there in Chicago?

In Example A, an estimated answer is enough. It is not necessary to know the exact cost of the items. All you need to know is that the total cost is not over $40. In Example B, an exact amount must be written on the check.

Practice

For each problem, first state whether an exact or estimated answer is necessary. Then solve the problem.

1. The owner of the store wants to keep at least 500 sweaters in stock at all times. She has sweaters on 3 racks. There are 185 sweaters on the first rack, 219 sweaters on the second rack, and 179 sweaters on the third rack. Does she need more sweaters in stock?

   Exact or Estimated? ____Estimated____   Answer: ____No.____

   (200 + 200 + 200 = 600)

2. Kyle bought two pairs of shoes during the BUY ONE—GET ONE HALF PRICE shoe sale. One pair cost $19.96. The other pair cost $23.95. How much did the two pairs of shoes cost before tax was added?

   Exact or Estimated? ____Exact____   Answer: ____$33.93____

   (23.95 + [19.96 ÷ 2] = 33.93)

3. Liz works in the store on Mondays, Wednesdays and Fridays. Last week she worked 7 hours 50 minutes on Monday, 6 hours 15 minutes on Wednesday, and 8 hours 45 minutes on Friday. About how many hours did Liz work last week?

   Exact or Estimated? ____Estimated____   Answer: ____about 23 hours____

   (8 + 6 + 9 = 23)

4. Pam has $50. Can she buy a jacket for $27.95, two pairs of socks for $3.15 each, and a shirt for $11.95?

   Exact or Estimated? ____Estimated____   Answer: ____Yes.____

   (28 + 3 + 3 + 12 = 46)

5. Will and Scott went shopping together. Will's bill was $39.95. He gave the clerk a 50-dollar bill. Scott's bill was $7.95. He gave the clerk a 20-dollar bill. Who received more change back from the clerk?

   Exact or Estimated? ____Estimated____   Answer: ____Scott did.____

   (50 − 40 = 10; 20 − 8 = 12)

6. Write a word problem of your own. Write a problem in which an estimated answer will be enough to solve the problem.

   Answers will vary, but check that an estimated answer will be enough

   to solve the problem. This would be a good item for class discussion.

Shoe Sale
Buy One—Get One Half Price
Buy one pair of shoes, get the second pair of equal or lesser value for half price.

More Than One Strategy

Aim: To recognize that there is often more than one way to solve a word problem

What You Need to Know

You have learned many strategies for solving word problems. Often, as soon as you read a problem, you will know which strategy to use. For routine problems, you simply add, subtract, multiply, or divide. For other problems, you may not be as sure what to do. If you try one strategy and it does not lead to a correct answer, reread the problem. Then try another strategy. Any strategy that gives you the correct answer is right for you!

Think About It

If you choose a strategy that doesn't work, what should you do?

Reread the problem and try another strategy.

Read each problem below. Notice the two strategies that are suggested for solving each.

Example A Ian is making lemonade. He needs 2 lemons for every 3 cups of water. How many cups of water should Ian put with the juice from 10 lemons?

Strategies:

Make a table.   *or*   *Use a ratio proportion.*

Lemons	2	4	6	8	10
Cups water	3	6	9	12	15

$\dfrac{2}{3} = \dfrac{10}{n}$ $2n = 30;$
$n = 15$

Answer: *15 cups of water*

Example B Sue walks $4\frac{1}{2}$ blocks to school. She started walking toward school and then remembered her homework. She walked back home for her homework and then walked to school. If she walked 6 blocks in all, how far had Sue walked before she remembered her homework?

Strategies:

Draw a diagram.   *or*   *Write an equation.*

$n + n + 4\frac{1}{2} = 6$
$2n + 4\frac{1}{2} = 6$
$2n = 1\frac{1}{2}$

Answer: $\frac{3}{4}$ *block* $n = \frac{3}{4}$

Making a table and using a ratio proportion are two strategies for Example A. You could also solve that problem by making a graph! Example B is solved by drawing a diagram or by writing an equation. You might even use both strategies. The picture makes it easier to see the action. That makes it easier to choose the correct operation for the equation.

Practice

Read each word problem. Choose a strategy to solve the problem. Then use your strategy to answer the question. Be sure to follow all five problem-solving steps.

1. Andy is putting 1-foot square tiles in his hallway. The hallway is 4 feet by 14 feet. The tile comes in boxes of 12 tiles each. How many boxes of tiles does he need to buy?

   Strategy: _Diagram (or formula)_   Answer: _5 boxes_
   ($4\frac{2}{3}$ boxes; round up)

2. A bus is traveling at a rate of 40 miles per hour. How long will it take the bus to travel 380 miles?

   Strategy: _Formula (or proportion)_   Answer: _$9\frac{1}{2}$ hours_

3. Juanita used 22 feet of fencing to make a triangular pen for her pet. One side of the pen is $10\frac{1}{2}$ feet. Another side is $5\frac{1}{4}$ feet. How long is the third side?

   Strategy: _Diagram (or equation)_   Answer: _$6\frac{3}{4}$ feet_

4. A 3-pound bag of apples costs $2.07. How much should you pay for 10 pounds of apples?

   Strategy: _Proportion (or table)_   Answer: _$6.90_

5. How many triangles are in this picture?

   Strategy: _Equation (or solve a simpler problem)_   Answer: _30 triangles_
   (6 new triangles in each of 5 "stages")

Additional word problems for Lesson 24 skills practice are on page 106.

57

Unit 3 Review

A. On each line, write **T** or **F** to tell whether the statement is true or false.

_T_ 1. If you have a problem that you are not sure how to solve, it may help to draw a diagram.

_F_ 2. After you make a line graph to solve a problem, you should make a table for the facts in the problem.

_T_ 3. Thinking about the actions in problems will help you to decide which operations to use.

_F_ 4. Only one correct equation can be used to solve a problem.

_T_ 5. If the numbers or situation make a problem seem difficult, it often helps to think of a similar but simpler problem.

_T_ 6. A proportion is true if the cross products are equal.

_F_ 7. "Puzzle" problems can usually be solved by adding or subtracting.

_T_ 8. A table often helps to organize the facts in a puzzle problem.

_F_ 9. You rarely need to find an exact answer to a word problem.

_F_ 10. As soon as you read a word problem, you will know the best strategy for solving it.

B. On each line, write the word that best completes the sentence.

line 11. If you want to find an unknown value that falls in between known values, or if you want to compare similar events, you can use a _____ graph.

variable 12. In an equation, a letter that can stand for different values is called a _____.

interest 13. In the formula $i = prt$, the letter i stands for _____.

proportion 14. An equation that states that two ratios are equal is called a _____.

estimated 15. When an exact answer to a problem is either not possible or not needed, you use an _____ answer.

C. Circle the letter of the correct answer.

16. Suppose 5 people are meeting each other. If each person shakes hands with every other person once, how many handshakes will there be?
    a. 8 handshakes   b. 20 handshakes   c. 10 handshakes   d. 15 handshakes

17. A train traveling at a constant speed travels 150 miles in 4 hours. How far will the train travel in 6 hours?
    a. 37.5 miles   b. 225 miles   c. 900 miles   d. 450 miles

18. Jay worked 30 hours last week. That was $6\frac{1}{2}$ hours more than Jean worked. How many hours did Jean work?
    a. $24\frac{1}{2}$ hours   b. $36\frac{1}{2}$ hours   c. 13 hours   d. $23\frac{1}{2}$ hours

19. Pat has 3 times as many coins as Sue has. Sue has 15 coins. How many coins does Pat have?
    a. 45 coins   b. 5 coins   c. 18 coins   d. 12 coins

20. A bus is traveling at a rate of 40 miles per hour. How long will it take the bus to travel 100 miles?
    a. 140 minutes   b. 60 minutes   c. $2\frac{1}{2}$ hours   d. 2 hours

21. Josh invested $100 at 6% simple interest for 5 years. How much interest did he earn?
    a. $20   b. $50   c. $30   d. $60

22. Raul has 12 small square tables. Each table can seat only one person on a side. Suppose the tables are pushed together to make one long table. How many people can sit at that long table?
    a. 48 people   b. 26 people   c. 24 people   d. 36 people

23. A map is drawn with a scale of 2 cm = 5 km. Suppose a road on the map measures 4 centimeters. How long is the actual road?
    a. 10 centimeters   b. 20 centimeters   c. 10 kilometers   d. 20 kilometers

24. These clues describe a number. What is the number?
    Clue 1: The number has 3 digits.
    Clue 2: The number is less than 200.
    Clue 3: The number can be divided evenly by 12 and by 9.
    Clue 4: The ones digit is less than the tens digit.
    a. 108   b. 216   c. 180   d. 132

25. Steve kept this record of the number of miles he jogged: Monday—$2\frac{1}{4}$ miles; Tuesday—$3\frac{3}{4}$ miles; Wednesday— $1\frac{1}{8}$ miles; Thursday—$3\frac{1}{4}$ miles; Friday—$2\frac{3}{4}$ miles. About how far did Steve jog in the 5 days?
    a. about 13 miles   b. about 17 miles   c. about 11 miles   d. about 15 miles

---

Go on to the next page.

D. Read and reread each word problem. Then follow the directions to show your solution to the problem.

26. An airplane is traveling at an average speed of (550 miles per hour.) About how far will the airplane travel in (3$\frac{1}{2}$ hours?)
    a. Underline the question.
    b. Circle the needed facts in the problem.

    c. Describe your plan: ___Use a formula: d = rt.___

    d. If an estimate can be made, show it here: ___600 × 3 = 1,800___

    e. Carry out your plan. Answer: ___1,925 miles___   (550 × 3.5 = 1,925)

    f. Check your answer. If you got an incorrect answer, tell how you know it is wrong. Then write the correct answer.

    ___Students who got incorrect answers should mention computation error or___

    ___that the answer was not reasonable.___

27. There are (32 students) in Mrs. Aplin's class. Suppose (3 out of 4 students walk to school.) How many students in Mrs. Aplin's class walk to school?
    a. Underline the question.
    b. Circle the needed facts in the problem.

    c. Describe your plan: ___Use a proportion.___

    d. If an estimate can be made, show it here: ___cannot be made___

    e. Carry out your plan. Answer: ___24 students___   ($\frac{3}{4}$ = $\frac{n}{32}$; 4n = 96; n = 24)

    f. Check your answer. If you got an incorrect answer, tell how you know it is wrong. Then write the correct answer.

    ___Students who got incorrect answers should mention computation error or___

    ___that the answer was not reasonable.___

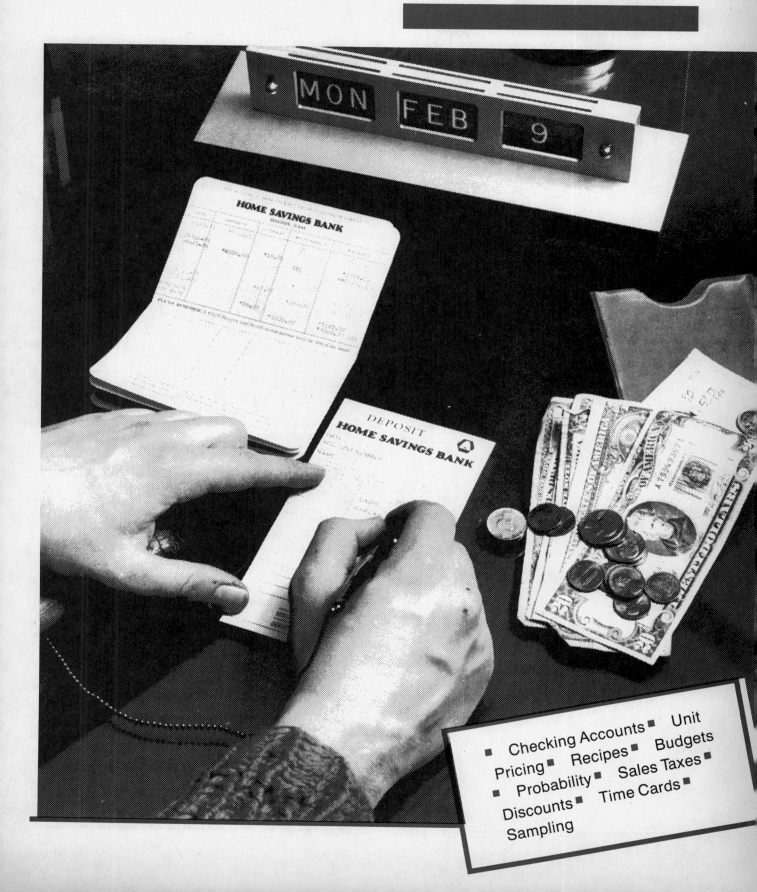

4 Applications

- Checking Accounts
- Unit Pricing
- Recipes
- Budgets
- Probability
- Sales Taxes
- Discounts
- Time Cards
- Sampling

Checking Accounts

What You Need to Know

When you have money in a bank **checking account,** you write *checks* to use the money. A *check register* is used to keep a record of the checks you write (the money you take out) and the deposits you make (the money you put in). The register shows the **balance,** or the amount of money left in the account. Each time you write a check, you subtract. Each time you make a deposit, you add.

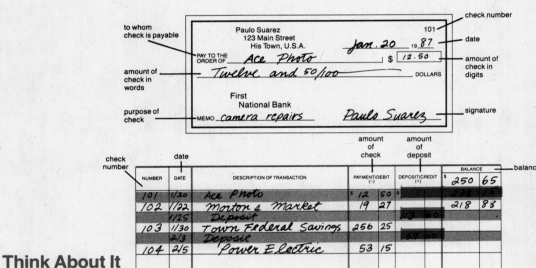

NUMBER	DATE	DESCRIPTION OF TRANSACTION	PAYMENT/DEBIT (−)	DEPOSIT/CREDIT (+)	BALANCE
					$ 250 65
101	1/20	Ace Photo	$ 12 50		
102	1/22	Morton's Market	19 27		218 88
	1/25	Deposit		113 60	
103	1/30	Town Federal Savings	256 25		
	2/3	Deposit			
104	2/5	Power Electric	53 15		

Think About It

After Paulo Suarez wrote check number 101, what was the balance

in his account? _____

Read the problems below. Notice where the facts are found.

Example A What was Paulo's balance after he made the deposit on January 25? Write the new balance on the register.

The Execution: 218.88
     + 113.60
     332.48

Answer: $332.48

Example B What was the balance after Paulo wrote check number 103? Write the new balance on the register.

The Execution: 332.48
     − 256.25
     76.23

Answer: $76.23

In Example A, Paulo is adding money to his checking account. So, you add to find the new balance. In Example B, you subtract to find the new balance. Paulo is using some of the money in his account to pay Town Federal Savings.

Practice

Answer these questions about checks and check registers.

1. May wrote a check for $27.35 on January 20, 1987. She made the check out to Bradley's Bookshop to pay for a dictionary. Complete May's check.

```
┌─────────────────────────────────────────────────────────────┐
│                                                               │
│   May Butler                                          101     │
│      456 Central Ave.                                         │
│      Her Town, U.S.A.        January 20  19 87                │
│                                                               │
│   PAY TO THE   Bradley's Bookshop            $   27.35        │
│   ORDER OF                                                    │
│              Twenty-seven and 35/00                           │
│                                                  DOLLARS      │
│                                                               │
│        Continental Bank                                       │
│                                                               │
│   MEMO   dictionary                    May Butler             │
│                                                               │
└─────────────────────────────────────────────────────────────┘
```

Use the check register on page 62 and the answers to Examples A and B to solve Practice items 2 and 3.

2. What was Paulo's balance after his deposit on February 3?

   $133.23   (76.23 + 57.00 = 133.23)

3. What was Paulo's balance after his check to Power Electric?

   $80.08   (133.23 − 53.15 = 80.08)

4. Janna had $413.60 in her checking account. On February 5, she wrote a check to The Sport Shop for $63.15. On February 7, she wrote a check to Fred's Garage for $125.20. How much money does Janna have left in her account after writing those 2 checks?

   $225.25   (413.60 − 63.15 = 350.45; 350.45 − 125.20 = 225.25)

5. This is Janna's check register. Complete the register for the checks Janna wrote in Practice item 4.

NUMBER	DATE	DESCRIPTION OF TRANSACTION	PAYMENT/DEBIT (−)		DEPOSIT/CREDIT (+)		BALANCE	
							$ 413	60
215	2/5	The Sport Shop	$ 63	15	$		350	45
216	2/7	Fred's Garage	125	20			225	25

Additional word problems for Lesson 25 skills practice are on page 107.

63

Unit Pricing

Aim: To solve problems by finding unit prices in order to determine "best buys"

What You Need to Know

Teacher Note: As students study the Examples, elicit the fact that using a calculator is probably the best way to compute when comparing prices to figure best buys. Depending on your class, you also may want to discuss what factors other than cost alone might go into determining a "best buy." In Example A, point out that the unit price is "per ounce," not "per nut."

To find the "best buy" when you shop, you can compare unit pricing. The unit price of an item can mean either:

- the price for one item, or
- the price for one unit of an item.

$$\text{unit price} = \frac{\text{total cost}}{\text{number of units}}$$

To find the best buy when shopping, use the above formula with each item. Compare the unit prices to find the best buy.

Think About It

How can finding unit prices help you to be a wise shopper?

You will be comparing costs for the same amounts.

Read the problems below. Notice how unit prices are found.

Example A   A 12-ounce can of nuts sells for $1.74. What is the unit price?

Formula: $\text{unit price} = \dfrac{\text{total cost}}{\text{number of units}}$

$$= \frac{1.74}{12}$$

$$= .145 \text{ or } .15 \text{ (rounded up)}$$

Answer: $0.15 per ounce

Example B   Look at the ads for apples. Which store has the better buy on apples?

Find the unit prices:

At Buy-Rite Foods: $\dfrac{1.45}{2} = .725$, rounding to $.73$

At Food Fair: $\dfrac{2.07}{3} = .69$

Compare the unit prices: $0.69 per pound is less than $0.73 per pound.

Answer: Food Fair has the better buy on apples.

Buy-Rite Foods
Apples
2 lb. $1.45

Food Fair
Apples
3 lb. $2.07

In Example A, the unit is an ounce. The unit price tells you that 1 ounce of nuts costs $0.15 (rounded to the nearest cent). In Example B, you find the best buy by comparing the unit prices of apples at two food stores. The unit is a pound.

Teacher Note: You may want to point out that finding unit prices may be accomplished using ratios as well as the unit-price formula practiced in this lesson. For example, in item 1, $\frac{5}{1} = \frac{.85}{n}$.

Practice

For items 1–4, find the unit price to the nearest cent.

1. 5 bars of soap for $0.85: ___$0.17 per bar of soap___   (0.85 ÷ 5 = 17)

2. 32 ounces of apple sauce for $1.12: ___$0.04 per ounce___
   (1.12 ÷ 32 = .035)

3. 4-pack of orange juice for $1.18: ___$0.30 per single container___
   (1.18 ÷ 4 = .295)

4. 1.5 pounds of cheese for $3.90: ___$2.60 per pound___
   (3.90 ÷ 1.5 = 2.60)

For Practice items 5–8, find the unit prices of the items. Then tell which is the better buy. For item 8, you will need to do one *more* step in order to answer the question.

5. 5-lb. bag of onions for $1.60 or 8-lb. bag of onions for $2.68

   Unit price for 5 lb.: ___$0.32 per pound___   (1.60 ÷ 5 = .32)

   Unit price for 8 lb.: ___$0.34 per pound___   (2.68 ÷ 8 = .335)

   Better Buy: ___5-lb. bag___

6. package of 8 rolls for $1.00 or package of 12 rolls for $1.32

   Unit price for 8 rolls: ___$0.13 per roll___   (1.00 ÷ 8 = .125)

   Unit price for 12 rolls: ___$0.11 per roll___   (1.32 ÷ 12 = .11)

   Better Buy: ___package of 12 rolls___

7. 20-oz. can of sliced pineapple for 78¢ or 7-oz. can for 35¢

   Unit price for 20-ounce can: ___$0.04 per ounce___   (.78 ÷ 20 = .039)

   Unit price for 7-ounce can: ___$0.05 per ounce___   (.35 ÷ 7 = .05)

   Better Buy: ___20-ounce can___

8. Two cans of Juicy Orange Juice sell for $1.78. Three cans of Tastee Orange Juice sell for $2.76. You buy 12 cans at the better buy. How much do you spend?

   Unit price for Juicy Juice: ___$0.89 per can___   (1.78 ÷ 2 = .89)

   Unit price for Tastee Juice: ___$0.92 per can___   (2.76 ÷ 3 = .92)

   Better Buy: ___Juicy Orange Juice___   Answer: ___$10.68___
   (.89 × 12 = 10.68)

Additional word problems for Lesson 26 skills practice are on page 108.

65

Recipes

What You Need to Know

A **recipe** tells how much of each item, or *ingredient,* to use, such as "2 cups" or "3 teaspoons." A recipe tells how much of each ingredient to use to serve a certain number of people. Sometimes you need to feed more or fewer people. Here is how to change a recipe's serving size:

- First, decide on the number of servings you need. (Example: You want to serve 4 people.)
- Second, compare this number with the number of servings for the recipe. Show this as a ratio written as a fraction. (Example: The recipe serves 3 people. The ratio is $\frac{4}{3}$.)
- Third, multiply *each ingredient amount in the recipe* by the ratio ($\frac{4}{3}$). The new amounts are the measures to use.

Think About It

What do you compare when you write a ratio to change a recipe?

You compare the servings you need to those in the recipe.

Notice how a ratio is used to solve each problem below.

Example A   Read Sue's recipe for meat loaf. Sue wants to prepare a meat loaf dinner for 12 people. How much ground beef does she need?

Sue's Meat Loaf	
$1\frac{1}{2}$ pounds ground beef	1 egg, beaten
1 cup bread crumbs	$\frac{1}{4}$ cup minced onion
$1\frac{1}{4}$ cups milk	$\frac{1}{2}$ teaspoon pepper

Mix all ingredients thoroughly. Spread in ungreased loaf pan 9″ x 5″ x 3″. Bake in 350° oven for $1\frac{1}{2}$ hours.

Serves 4

Ratio: $\dfrac{servings\ needed}{servings\ in\ recipe} = \dfrac{12}{4}$, *or 3*

The Execution: *needed amount = ratio × recipe amount*
needed amount ground beef = 3 × $1\frac{1}{2}$ = $4\frac{1}{2}$

Answer: $4\frac{1}{2}$ *pounds*

Example B   How much onion is needed to make a meat loaf for 2 people?

Ratio: $\dfrac{servings\ needed}{servings\ in\ recipe} = \dfrac{2}{4} = \dfrac{1}{2}$

The Execution: *needed amount = ratio × recipe amount*
needed amount onions = $\frac{1}{2}$ × $\frac{1}{4}$ = $\frac{1}{8}$

Answer: $\frac{1}{8}$ *cup*

In Example A, the ratio comparing the servings needed to the servings in the recipe is $\frac{12}{4}$, or 3. Sue wants to serve three times as many people as the recipe serves. She must triple the recipe. She must multiply the amount of each ingredient by 3.

In Example B, the ratio is $\frac{2}{4}$ or $\frac{1}{2}$. Sue wants to serve $\frac{1}{2}$ as many people as the recipe serves. She must multiply the amount of each ingredient by $\frac{1}{2}$.

Practice

Solve each problem using the facts in the recipes. Show the ratio and the answer.

1. What amount of bread crumbs would Sue need to make meat loaf for 6 people?

   Ratio: __$\frac{6}{4}$ or $\frac{3}{2}$__   Answer: __$\frac{3}{2}$ cups, or $1\frac{1}{2}$ cups__

   $(\frac{3}{2} \times 1 = \frac{3}{2})$

2. How much milk would Sue use to make meat loaf for 2 people?

   Ratio: __$\frac{2}{4}$__   Answer: __$\frac{5}{8}$ cup__ $(\frac{1}{2} \times 1\frac{1}{4} = \frac{5}{8})$

Banana Oatmeal Muffins	
2 eggs	1 cup oats
$\frac{1}{2}$ cup cooking oil	$\frac{1}{4}$ cup wheat germ
1 cup mashed bananas	$\frac{3}{4}$ cup whole wheat flour
$\frac{3}{4}$ cup honey	1 teaspoon baking powder
	1 teaspoon baking soda
Sift together flour, baking powder, and baking soda. Set aside. Beat oil and eggs. Add bananas to egg mixture. Add honey and flour mixture, blending by hand. Stir in oats and wheat germ. Fill muffin cups $\frac{2}{3}$ full. Bake at 375° for 20 minutes.	
	Makes 18 muffins

3. How much whole wheat flour would you use to make 36 muffins?

   Ratio: __$\frac{36}{18}$ or 2__   Answer: __$1\frac{1}{2}$ cups__ $(2 \times \frac{3}{4} = \frac{6}{4})$

4. How much wheat germ would you use to make 12 muffins?

   Ratio: __$\frac{12}{18} = \frac{2}{3}$__   Answer: __$\frac{1}{6}$ cup__ $(\frac{2}{3} \times \frac{1}{4} = \frac{1}{6})$

5. Suppose you have only 1 egg. How many muffins can you make? (Hint: Compare eggs you have with eggs you need to form a ratio.)

   Ratio: __$\frac{1}{2}$__   Answer: __9 muffins__ $(\frac{1}{2} \times 18 = 9)$

Additional word problems for Lesson 27 skills practice are on page 109.

Budgets

What You Need to Know

A **budget** is a plan for using money. It helps people or companies to use their money wisely. A **circle graph** can help you to "see" all parts of a budget. The graph makes it easy to compare the amounts of money to be spent in various areas.

The facts shown on a circle graph usually are shown in **percents.** The sum of all percents should be 100%. The greater the percent, the greater the region in the graph.

Think About It

Teacher Note: Have students add the percents in the circle graph, seeing that they total 100%.

Study the circle graph on this page. What is its title?

"Gina's Budget"

Gina's Budget

Read each problem. Notice where the information is found in the circle graph to help answer each question.

Example A   Gina has a part-time job at a grocery store. The circle graph shows how she decided to budget the money she earns. Last week Gina earned $84. How much money should she have put away as savings last week?

Needed Graph Facts: *25% for savings*

The Plan: Find 25% of $84.

The Execution:

$$\begin{array}{r} 84 \\ \times\ .25 \\ \hline 420 \\ 168 \\ \hline 21.00 \end{array}$$

Answer: $21

Example B   This week Gina earned $72. She wants to buy a new jacket. The jacket costs $34.99. If she spends only the money she has budgeted for clothing this week, can she buy the jacket?

Needed Graph Facts: *30% for clothing*

The Plan: *Find 30% of 72.*

The Execution:

$$\begin{array}{r} 72 \\ \times\ .30 \\ \hline 21.60 \end{array}$$

Answer: *No, she cannot buy the jacket.*

In Example A, the needed fact in the graph is found in the region for "savings." Gina budgeted 25% of her earnings for savings. So, take 25% of $84 to find the amount of money budgeted to be saved for that week.

In Example B, the information in the graph is found in the region for "clothes." To answer the question, compare the amount budgeted for clothes ($21.60) to the cost of the jacket ($34.99).

Teacher Note: Some students may state a different "Plan" for solving Practice items 4 and 5. Item 4 may be solved by adding 20% of $36,000 to 15% of $36,000. Item 5 may be solved by subtracting 10% of $36,000 from 15% of $36,000.

Practice

For each problem, write the needed graph facts, the plan, and the answer. Use the circle graph on page 68 for items 1 and 2.

1. If Gina earns $92, how much can she spend on lunches?

Needed Graph Facts: _____ 15% for lunches _____

The Plan: _____ Find 15% of $92. _____ Answer: _____ $13.80 _____
(.15 × 92 = 13.80)

2. In February, Gina earned $344. She wants to buy a new camera. The camera costs $75. Can Gina buy the camera with the money she budgeted for savings in February?

Needed Graph Facts: _____ 25% for savings _____

The Plan: _____ Find 25% of 344. _____ Answer: _____ Yes _____
(.25 × 344 = 86)

Mr. and Mrs. Simon's combined take-home pay is $36,000 a year. They made this graph to show how they plan to budget their money.

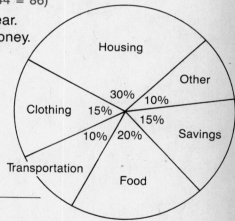

3. How much money have Mr. and Mrs. Simon budgeted for housing?

Needed Graph Facts: _____ 30% for housing _____

The Plan: _____ Find 30% of $36,000. _____ Answer: _____ $10,800 _____
(.30 × 36,000 = 10,800)

4. How much money have Mr. and Mrs. Simon budgeted for food and clothing together?

Needed Graph Facts: _____ 35% for food and clothing (20% + 15% = 35%) _____

The Plan: _____ Find 35% of $36,000. _____ Answer: _____ $12,600 _____
(.35 × 36,000 = 12,600)

5. How much more money have Mr. and Mrs. Simon budgeted for savings than for transportation?

Needed Graph Facts: _____ 5% more for savings _____

The Plan: _____ Find 5% of $36,000. _____ Answer: _____ $1,800 _____
(.05 × 36,000 = 1,800)

Additional word problems for Lesson 28 skills practice are on page 110.

69

Probability

What You Need to Know

"Spinners" are often used in games of chance. Suppose you want to know your chance, or likelihood, for spinning a certain number. You would find your chance by finding the **probability** of spinning that number.

Probability is a number from 0 to 1. It tells how likely it is that an event will happen. Look at the spinner on this page.

- There are six *possible outcomes* on the spinner.
- Each region is the same size. So, the spinner is *equally likely* to stop in any one region.
- If you want to spin a 4, then spinning a 4 is called the *favorable outcome.*

To find the probability of something happening, use this formula:

$$\text{probability} = \frac{\text{number of favorable outcomes}}{\text{number of possible outcomes}}$$

Only one region on the spinner has a 4. So, there is only 1 favorable outcome. There are six regions on the spinner. So, there are 6 possible outcomes. The probability of spinning a 4 is $\frac{1}{6}$.

Think About It

Teacher Note: Be sure students understand, when answering the question under "Think About It," that the probability of spinning any single number from 1 to 6 on the spinner is the same, $\frac{1}{6}$.

What is the probability of spinning a 6?

$\frac{1}{6}$

Read each problem. Use the spinner on this page for both Examples. Notice how the favorable outcomes and the possible outcomes are found.

Example A   Find the probability of spinning a number greater than 4.
Number of Favorable Outcomes: *2*
Number of Possible Outcomes: *6*
Probability: $\frac{2}{6}$, *or* $\frac{1}{3}$

Example B   Find the probability of spinning a number less than 5.
Number of Favorable Outcomes: *4*
Number of Possible Outcomes: *6*
Probability: $\frac{4}{6}$, *or* $\frac{2}{3}$

In Example A, there are two regions on the spinner carrying numbers greater than 4. These are the regions for 5 and 6. So, there are 2 favorable outcomes. There are six regions in all, so there are 6 possible outcomes.

In Example B, there are 4 favorable outcomes. The regions for 1, 2, 3, and 4 are all less than 5. Again, there are 6 possible outcomes.

Teacher Note: Elicit from students that there can never be more favorable outcomes than there are possible outcomes. That is why probability is **Practice** never a number greater than 1.

Remember to follow all five problem solving steps as you solve these probability problems.

| O | U | T | C | O | M | E | S |

The letter-cards shown here are placed in a bag. Each card is made of the same material. Each card is shaped exactly the same. One card is picked without looking. Answer questions 1–4 about the drawings of letter-cards.

1. What is the probability of picking a T? $\frac{1}{8}$

2. What is the probability of picking an O? $\frac{2}{8}$, or $\frac{1}{4}$

3. What is the probability of picking an O, U, or C? $\frac{4}{8}$, or $\frac{1}{2}$

4. What is the probability of picking an A? $\frac{0}{8}$, or 0

5. There are 6 red marbles, 3 green marbles, and 1 blue marble in a jar. They are all the same except in color. You reach in the jar without looking and pick one marble. What is the probability of picking a green marble?

    $\frac{3}{10}$

6. You toss a coin. What is the probability it lands on "heads"?

    $\frac{1}{2}$

7. The numbers 1 through 6 are on a number cube. The cube is rolled. What is the probability of rolling an even number?

    $\frac{3}{6}$ or $\frac{1}{2}$

Additional word problems for Lesson 29 skills practice are on page 111.

Sales Tax

Aim: To solve problems by finding the sales tax on items
and then computing the total cost

What You Need to Know

 Cities and states need money to provide services. Their services
include schools, police and fire departments, parks, libraries, and
activity centers. One way to raise this money is to collect a tax. A
sales tax is an amount of money added to the price of something
you buy.

Use these formulas to find the amount of sales tax and then the
total cost of an item. The rate of a sales tax is usually given as a
percent.

sales tax = rate of sales tax × price of item

total cost = price + sales tax

Think About It

How is a sales tax rate usually shown? ___It is shown as a percent.___

Read each Example. Remember, when using a percent in a mathematical operation, change it to a decimal.

Example A Saul is buying a basketball for $12.50 plus 5% tax. What
is the total cost of the basketball?

Sales Tax: 12.50	**Total Cost:** 12.50
× .05	+ .63
.6250, rounded up to .63	13.13

Answer: $13.13

Example B Peggy has $20. She wants to buy a baseball bat that
costs $12.95 and a baseball that costs $5.95. There is a
6% sales tax. Can she buy the bat and ball?

Price of Items: 12.95	**Sales Tax:** 18.90
+ 5.95	× .06
18.90	1.1340
	rounded down 1.13

Total Cost: 18.90
+ 1.13
20.03

Answer: *No, she cannot.*

In Example A, the sales tax rate (5%) is changed to a decimal (.05) before computing the amount of the sales tax. Notice that $.625 is rounded up to the nearest whole cent, $.63. The total cost is found by adding the price ($12.50) and the sales tax ($.63).

In Example B, the price of the bat and ball is found *before* computing the sales tax. The total cost is $20.03. Since Peggy has only $20, she cannot buy the bat and ball.

Teacher Note: Some students may be aware that the total cost can also be computed in one step. A $3.50 item with a 5% sales tax, for instance, may be computed as 3.50 × 1.05 = 3.675, or $3.68 total cost.

Practice

Solve each problem. Read the question carefully! Sometimes, you will need to find the amount of sales tax. Other times, you will need to find the total cost.

1. The price of a pair of jogging shoes is $32.95. The sales tax is 6%. Find the amount of tax.

   $1.98   (32.95 × .06 = 1.977)

2. Maria bought a warm-up jacket for $29.95 plus 4% sales tax. What was her total cost?

   $31.15   (29.95 × .04 = 1.198; 29.95 + 1.20 = 31.15)

3. Tracy has $8. Can she buy swimming goggles that cost $7.50 plus 5% sales tax?

   Yes, she can.   (7.50 × .05 = .375; 7.50 + .38 = 7.88)

4. Frank wants to buy a tennis racket for $19.95 and a can of tennis balls for $2.99. There is a 5% sales tax. What will be the total cost of the racket and can of balls?

   Answer: $24.09   (19.95 + 2.99 = 22.94; 22.94 × .05 = 1.147; 22.94 + 1.15 = 24.09)

5. Steven bought a football for $21.50. Phil bought a soccer ball for $16.95. There is a 6% sales tax. How much more did Steven spend than Phil?

   Answer: $4.82

   (Steven: 21.50 × .06 = 1.29; 21.50 + 1.29 = 22.79)
   (Phil: 16.95 × .06 = 1.017; 16.95 + 1.02 = 17.97; 22.79 – 17.97 = 4.82)

Discounts

What You Need to Know

At times a store will offer a **discount**. A discount is an amount of money that is subtracted from the original selling price. When you buy something on a discount, you pay less than usual. As with a sales tax, the rate of a discount is usually given as a percent. Use these formulas to find the amount of discount and the sale price.

discount = rate of discount × original price
sale price = original price − discount

Think About It

How do you find the discount on an item? _____ Multiply the original price

by the rate of discount.

Read each problem. Notice how the discount rate is changed from a percent to a decimal before multiplying.

the STEREO SHOP

One day only!! CLOSE-OUT SALE

15—30% off

| blank tapes | 15% off | jazz tapes classical tapes } | 20% off |
| rock tapes country/western tapes } | 25% off | all others | 30% off |

Example A The Stereo Shop is having a one-day closeout sale on all its tapes. During the sale, Kate bought a rock tape that had an original price of $8.65. What was the sale price of the tape?

Discount: 8.65   Sale Price: 8.65
         × .25   − 2.16
         2.1625, rounded down 2.16   6.49

Answer: $6.49

Example B Records are also on sale at the Stereo Shop. Tina bought a record that was $3.00 off the original price of $7.50. What was the percent of discount?

Use Discount Formula for Different Purpose:
discount = rate of discount × original price
3.00 = n × 7.50
$\frac{3.00}{7.50}$ = n = .4   **Answer:** 40%

In Example A, 25% is changed to .25 for use in the formula for finding the discount. Then the discount is subtracted from the original price to find the sale price.

In Example B, the formula for finding the discount is used again. This time, however, the formula is used to find the rate of discount, or the percent. Substitute the known values in the equation. Solve for the unknown value, *n*.

Practice

Solve each problem. Read the questions carefully!

1. Tim bought a jazz tape that originally sold for $4.50. What was the discount?

   $.90   (4.50 × .20 = .90)

2. Anita bought a blank tape during the sale. The original price was $3.50. What was the sale price?

   $2.97   (3.50 × .15 = .525; 3.50 − .53 = 2.97)

3. Jim bought a blank tape that originally sold for $3.00. He also bought a country/western tape that originally sold for $6.25. What was the sale price of the two tapes together?

   $7.24   (3.00 × .15 = .45; 3.00 − .45 = 2.55; 6.25 × .25 = 1.5625; 6.25 − 1.56 = 4.69; 2.55 + 4.69 = 7.24)

4. Earphones are on sale for $5 off the original price of $20. What is the percent of discount? (Hint: Look at Example B.)

   25%   (5 = n × 20; n = .25)

5. A stereo radio is on sale for $60. The original price was $75. What is the percent of discount? (Hint: First find the amount of discount.)

   20%   (75 − 60 = 15; 15 = n × 75; n = .2)

Additional word problems for Lesson 31 skills practice are on page 113.

Time Cards

What You Need to Know

A **time card** is a table set up to record the number of hours worked. Some workers get an **overtime rate** if they work more than the normal number of hours. Often, overtime is paid at "time and a half." This means the worker earns 1.5 times the normal hourly rate for each hour of overtime he or she works. The total amount earned is the sum of the overtime pay and the regular pay.

MAIN ST. SALON—Time Card

Name _Clay Osborne_

Week Ending _April 30_

	In	Out		In	Out	Hours Worked
Sun.						
Mon.	8:00	11:30	LUNCH	12:00	4:00	$7\frac{1}{2}$
Tues.	10:00	12:00	LUNCH	12:30	7:00	$8\frac{1}{2}$
Sat.	9:00	12:30		1:00	6:00	$8\frac{1}{2}$
					Total Hours	45

Think About It

How many hours did Clay work Tuesday? How many hours all week?

He worked $8\frac{1}{2}$ hours Tuesday and 45 hours all week.

Read each problem. Notice how Clay's pay is calculated.

Example A   Clay earns $5.50/hour. He gets time and a half for overtime. How much is he paid per hour of overtime?

The Plan: _1.5 × regular hourly pay = overtime pay_

The Execution: 5.50   **Answer: $8.25**
                    × 1.5
                    ─────
                    2750
                    550
                    ─────
                    8.250

Example B   Clay is paid overtime for work over 40 hours in a week. How much did he earn the week ending April 30?

The Plan: _regular pay + overtime pay = total pay_

The Execution: 5.50   8.25   220.00   **Answer:**
                     × 40   × 5   + 41.25 $261.25
                    ──────   ─────   ───────
                     220.00   41.25   261.25

In Example A, multiply Clay's regular hourly pay by 1.5 to find his overtime hourly pay. In Example B, first find the amount Clay earned for the 40 hours worked at regular hourly pay. Then find the amount earned for the 5 hours of overtime. Clay's total weekly pay is the sum of his regular and his overtime pay.

Practice

Answer the questions about each time card.

1. Rosa earns $6.25 per hour at Best-Buy Food Mart. She is paid time and a half for overtime. How much does she earn for each hour of overtime?

$9.38　　　　　(6.25 × 1.5 = 9.375)

BEST-BUY FOOD MART—Time Card

Name _Rosa Duke_

Week Ending _May 30_

	In	Out		In	Out	Hours Worked
Sun.						
Mon.	8:00	12:00	LUNCH	1:00	4:00	7
Tues.	9:00	1:00		1:30	4:30	7
Wed.	8:30	12:30		1:30	5:30	8
Thurs.	9:00	1:00		2:00	5:00	7
Fri.	10:00	2:00		3:00	7:00	8
Sat.	10:30	1:00				2.5
					Total Hours	39.5

2. Rosa is paid overtime for the time over 35 hours that she works. How much did Rosa earn during the week ending May 30?

$260.96　(6.25 × 35 = 218.75; 9.38 × 4.5 = 42.21; 218.75 + 42.21 = 260.96)

3. Complete the "Hours Worked" column on the card for Mel Thomas.

4. Mel earns $10.50 per hour. He is paid time and a half for overtime. How much does he earn for each hour of overtime?

$15.75　　　　　(10.50 × 1.5 = 15.75)

AUTO WORKS—Time Card

Name _Mel Thomas_

Week Ending _June 30_

	In	Out		In	Out	Hours Worked
Sun.						
Mon.	7:00	11:30	LUNCH	12:30	4:30	8½
Tues.	8:00	12:00		1:00	6:00	9
Wed.	7:00	11:00		12:00	4:30	8½
Thurs.	7:00	11:30		12:30	4:00	8
Fri.	7:00	12:00		1:00	3:00	7
Sat.	8:00	12:00				4
					Total Hours	45

5. Mel is paid overtime for the time over 40 hours that he works. How much did Mel earn during the week ending June 30?

$498.75　　　(10.50 × 40 = 420; 15.75 × 5 = 78.75; 420 + 78.75 = 498.75)

Additional word problems for Lesson 32 skills practice are on page 114.

Sampling

Aim: To solve problems by making predictions based on samples

What You Need to Know

Sometimes you can use a **sample** of a group to answer questions about the whole group. This is done when it would be too hard (or not possible) to survey the whole group.

- To predict who will win an election, a newspaper may sample a group of voters.
- To decide what songs to play, a radio station may sample a group of listeners.

When a sample is used to make a prediction about a larger group, the sample must be *unbiased.* That is, it must truly reflect the whole group. Members of the sample must be picked at *random.*

Teacher Note: Make sure students understand that when members of a sample are picked "at random," then each member has an *equal probability* of being picked.

Think About It

Suppose you wanted to learn the favorite sport of the students in your school. Which of these methods of picking people to ask would be biased: every third person in the hall or every fifth person in the stands at a basketball game?

every fifth person in the stands at a basketball game

Read each problem. Notice how the percent is found and then used to make a prediction.

Favorite Music

popular		25
country	ЖТ	5
jazz	ЖТ ЖТ	10
classical	//	2
other	ЖТ ///	8

Example A   The school newspaper asked 50 randomly selected students to name their favorite kind of music. The results are shown in the chart. What percent of the students chose country music?

The Plan and Execution:

$$\frac{\text{students choosing country music}}{\text{students in sample}} \times 100 = percent$$

$$\frac{5}{50} = \frac{1}{10} = .10 \qquad .10 \times 100 = 10$$

Answer: *10%*

Example B   There are 890 students in the school. Based on the sample, how many students in the school like country music best?

The Plan and Execution: *10% of 890 (.10 × 890 = 89)*

Answer: *89 students*

In Example A, you find what percent of a sample answered a certain way. Once you know how a sample breaks down into percents, you can apply this breakdown to the whole group. (The whole group here is all the students in the school.) So, in Example B, you can say how many members of the whole group would answer in each category.

Practice

1. What percent of students in the sample on page 78 like popular music best?

   50% $(^{25}/_{50} = \frac{1}{2} = 50\%)$

2. There are 890 students in the school. Based on the sample, how many students in the school like popular music best?

   445 students $(890 \times .50 = 445)$

3. In a random sample of 30 students, 6 walk to school. Based on this sample, how many of the 890 students can you predict walk to school?

   178 students $(^{6}/_{30} = \frac{1}{5} \text{ or } 20\%; .20 \times 890 = 178)$

CITY GAZETTE
Poll Results

Gomez	35
Hillard	55
Undecided	10

4. The local newspaper asked 100 voters for whom they planned to vote for city mayor. The results are shown in the chart. Based on the poll results, how many votes would you expect Hillard to receive if 15,000 people vote in the election?

   8,250 votes $(^{55}/_{100} = 55\%; .55 \times 15,000 = 8,250)$

5. In a random sample of 50 students, 6 said they were going to try out for the school band. There are 725 students in the school. Based on the sample, how many students can you predict will try out for the school band?

   87 students $(^{6}/_{50} = 12\%; .12 \times 725 = 87)$

Unit 4 Review

A. On each line, write **T** or **F** to tell whether the statement is true or false.

___F___ **1.** Each time you write a check, you should add that amount of money to the balance in your checking account.

___T___ **2.** To find the "best buy" when shopping, you need to compare unit prices.

___T___ **3.** When you write a ratio to change a recipe, you compare the servings you need to the servings in the recipe.

___T___ **4.** A circle graph can help you to "see" a budget.

___F___ **5.** The sum of all the percents in a circle graph should be 50%.

___F___ **6.** Probability is a number between 0 and 100.

___F___ **7.** A sales tax is an amount of money subtracted from the price of something you buy.

___T___ **8.** To find the discount on an item, multiply the original price by the rate of the discount.

___F___ **9.** An overtime rate is paid to workers who have worked for a company for more than 1 year.

___T___ **10.** Sometimes you can use a sample of a group to answer questions about the whole group.

B. On each line, write the word that best completes the sentence.

___register___ **11.** A record of the checks you write and the deposits you make in your checking account is kept in a check _____.

___unit price___ **12.** The cost of one item, or the cost of one unit of an item, is called the _____ _____.

___budget___ **13.** A plan for using money is called a _____.

___probability___ **14.** A number that tells how likely it is that an event will happen is called a _____.

___hours___ **15.** A time card is a table set up to record the number of _____ worked.

C. Circle the letter of the correct answer.

16. Doug had $250 in his checking account. He wrote a check for $23. How much money does he have in his checking account now?

    a. $273   **b.** $227   **c.** $233   **d.** $250

17. Katy had $415.25 in her checking account. She made a deposit of $35.13 into her checking account. How much money does she have in her checking account now?

    a. $440.38   **b.** $380.12   **c.** $450.38   **d.** $420.12

18. Find the unit price of potatoes if a 5-lb. bag of potatoes costs $1.20.

    a. $0.24 per pound   **b.** $0.24 per potato   **c.** $0.24 per bag   **d.** $0.24 per ounce

> **Waldorf Salad**
> 1 cup diced celery
> 2 apples, diced
> $\frac{1}{2}$ cup walnut pieces
> $\frac{1}{2}$ cup mayonnaise
> juice of 1 lemon
>
> Mix ingredients.   Serves 4.

Wendy's Budget

19. How many apples are needed to make Waldorf salad for 12?

    a. 4 apples   **b.** 12 apples   **c.** 8 apples   **d.** 6 apples

20. Last week, Wendy earned $120. If she followed her budget, how much money did Wendy put away for savings?

    a. $36   **b.** $120   **c.** $30   **d.** $12

21. The numbers 1 through 6 are on a number cube. The cube is rolled. What is the probability of a 3 landing face up?

    a. $\frac{3}{6}$ **b.** $\frac{6}{6}$ **c.** $\frac{1}{6}$ **d.** $\frac{0}{6}$

22. Carla is buying a tennis racket for $35.95 plus 5% sales tax. What is the total cost of the tennis racket?

    a. $1.80   **b.** $34.15   **c.** $37.75   **d.** $36.75

23. Luis bought a book on sale for 25% off the original price. The original price was $7.80. What was the sale price?

    a. $1.95   **b.** $5.85   **c.** $9.75   **d.** $6.15

24. Liz earns $6.50/hour. She gets time and a half for time over 40 hours that she works. One week, Liz worked 43 hours. How much did she earn that week?

    a. $279.50   **b.** $419.25   **c.** $260.00   **d.** $289.25

25. In a random sample of 50 students, 30 students had pet dogs. There are 750 students in the school. Based on the sample, how many students in the school have pet dogs?

    a. 450 students   **b.** 550 students   **c.** 225 students   **d.** 425 students

Unit 4 Review (Continued)

D. Read and reread each word problem. Then follow the directions to show your solution to the problem.

Buy-Rite Foods
Applesauce
28-ounce jar
$1.12

Food Fair
Applesauce
16-ounce jar
$0.80

26. Look at the ads for applesauce. <u>Which store has the better buy on applesauce?</u>

  a. Underline the question.

  b. Circle the needed facts in the problem.

  c. Describe your plan: <u>Find unit prices to determine the better buy.</u>

  d. If an estimate can be made, show it here: <u>cannot be made</u>

  e. Carry out your plan. Answer: <u>Buy-Rite Foods has the better buy. (Its unit price is 4¢/oz., compared with Food Fair's 5¢/oz.: 1.12 ÷ 28 = .04; .80 ÷ 16 = .05)</u>

  f. Check your answer. If you got an incorrect answer, tell how you know it is wrong. Then write the correct answer.

  Students who got incorrect answers should mention computation error or that the answer was not reasonable.

27. Henry is buying a jacket for $39. There is a 5% sales tax. <u>What is the total cost of the jacket?</u>

  a. Underline the question.

  b. Circle the needed facts in the problem.

  c. Describe your plan: <u>Find the total cost. (Total cost = price of item + sales tax; sales tax = rate × price of item)</u>

  d. If an estimate can be made, show it here: <u>cannot be made</u>

  e. Carry out your plan. Answer: <u>$40.95 (.05 × 39 = 1.95; 39 + 1.95 = 40.95)</u>

  f. Check your answer. If you got an incorrect answer, tell how you know it is wrong. Then write the correct answer.

  Students who got incorrect answers should mention computation error or that the answer was not reasonable.

Step One: Read the Problem
(pages 2–3)

Guided-Tour Tickets	
adults	$2.50
children	
6–12	$1.25
under 6	free

Reword the question in each of the following word problems.

1. There are 75 people waiting to ride the elevator to the top of the city's tallest building. Only 30 people may ride on each trip. How many trips must the elevator make?

   The Question: How many trips, with 30 people in each trip, will the elevator have to make to carry 75 people?   (3 trips)

2. Guided tours of the building are given. Mr. Randall bought two adult tickets. How much did he spend?

   The Question: How much do two adult tickets cost?

   ($5.00)

3. Mr. Chin went on the tour with his 8-year-old daughter and his 4-year-old son. How much did Mr. Chin spend for tickets?

   The Question: How much do one adult ticket and one children's ticket cost?   ($3.75)

4. One tour began at 1:15 P.M. and ended at 1:55 P.M. How long did the tour last?

   The Question: How many minutes is it between 1:15 P.M. and 1:55 P.M.?

   (40 minutes)

5. Guidebooks cost $1.25. Rosa bought 3 guidebooks. How much did she spend?

   The Question: What is the total cost of 3 books if each book costs $1.25?

   ($3.75)

6. There are plans to build 15 new buildings on 5 city blocks. The same number of buildings will be built on each block. How many buildings will be built on each block?

   The Question: If 15 buildings are distributed evenly in 5 blocks, how many buildings are in each block?   (3 buildings)

7. Each story in a building is about 12 feet high. About how tall will the 78-story building be?

   The Question: How many feet tall is a building that has 78 stories if each story is 12 feet high?   (936 feet)

Step Two: Find the Facts

(pages 4–5)

Teacher Note: Although students are not asked to solve the problems, many students will do so. Answers to the problems are included for your information.

For each word problem, underline the question. Then write the facts you need to solve the problem.

1. Hobby Outlet sells three balls of twine for $0.81 and three skeins of yarn for $1.77. <u>How much does one ball of twine cost?</u>

   The Facts: _____ Cost of 3 balls of twine: $0.81 _____

   ($0.27)

2. Saturday, 193 people came into the store. Of those, 76 people made purchases. <u>How many people came into the store and did not buy anything?</u>

   The Facts: _____ Number of people in store: 193 _____

   Number of people who made purchases: 76   (117 people)

3. Max lives $4\frac{1}{4}$ miles from the Hobby Outlet. Ahmed lives $2\frac{1}{2}$ miles from the Hobby Outlet. Max rode his bike to the Outlet and then back home. <u>How far did Max ride in all?</u>

   The Facts: _____ Distance Max lives from store: $4\frac{1}{4}$ miles _____

   ($8\frac{1}{2}$ miles)

BEAD SALE

	Regular Price	Sale Price
Plastic		
large	.24	.12
medium	.18	.09
Wooden		
large	.15	.09
medium	.12	.07

4. Rhonda bought 12 large wooden beads during the bead sale. <u>How much did the beads cost?</u>

   The Facts: _____ Number of beads bought: 12 _____

   Cost of one bead: $0.09   ($1.08)

5. Last week, Joe paid the regular price for 10 large plastic beads. This week, he bought 10 more for the sale price. <u>How much more did he pay for the beads last week?</u>

   The Facts: _____ Number of beads: 10   Cost of beads on sale: $0.12 _____

   Regular price of beads: $0.24   ($1.20 more)

6. The Hobby Outlet is open from 9 A.M. to 9 P.M. on Monday through Saturday and from noon to 5 P.M. on Sunday. <u>For how many hours is the store open in 1 week?</u>

   The Facts: _____ Number of days: 6   Hours Open: 9 A.M. to 9 P.M. _____

   Number of days: 1   Hours Open: noon to 5 P.M.   (77 hours)

84

Step Three: Plan What to Do
(pages 6–7)

For each problem, underline the question. Circle the needed facts. Then write a plan for solving the problem. Estimate the answer, if possible.

1. Mr. Gomez teaches 2 woodworking classes. There are 43 students in the 2 classes. There are 24 students in one class. How many students are in the other class?

   The Plan: Subtract (total number of students − students in one class = students in other class)

   The Estimate: 40 − 20 = 20   (19 students)

2. Each of the 43 students did 4 projects during the school year. How many projects were done by all the students during the year?

   The Plan: Multiply (number of students × number of projects per student = total number of projects)

   The Estimate: 40 × 4 = 160   (172 projects)

3. Nancy has a board that is $7\frac{1}{2}$ feet long. She wants to cut the board to make 3 shelves that are the same length. How long will each shelf be?

   The Plan: Divide (total length of board ÷ number of shelves = length of each shelf)

   The Estimate: 8 ÷ 3 = $2\frac{2}{3}$ ($2\frac{1}{2}$ feet)

4. Julie spent 14 hours working on one project. She worked for $9\frac{3}{4}$ hours during class time and the rest of the time after school. How much time did Julie spend on her project after school?

   The Plan: Subtract (total number of hours − number of hours in class = number of hours after school)

   The Estimate: 14 − 10 = 4   ($4\frac{1}{4}$ hours)

5. New ceiling tiles are being installed in the woodworking classroom. The classroom is 32 feet wide by 48 feet long. How many square feet of tile are needed for the ceiling?

   The Plan: Use a formula: A = lw (area = length × width)

   The Estimate: 30 × 50 = 1,500   (1,536 sq. ft.)

6. Marie cut a $27\frac{3}{8}$-inch piece from a board that was 1 yard long. How long was the piece of board that was left?

   The Plan: Subtract (total number of inches − number of inches cut off = number of inches left)

   The Estimate: 36 − 27 = 9   ($8\frac{5}{8}$ inches)

Step Four: Carry Out the Plan
(pages 8–9)

Solve each problem. Be sure to follow all the steps you have learned.

91 pairs
_____

1. Tim sells shoes at the Shoe Shop. He sold 52 pairs of shoes on Monday and 39 pairs on Tuesday. How many pairs did he sell in all on those 2 days?

18 more pairs
_____

2. Tim will earn a special bonus if he sells 75 pairs of boots. He has already sold 57 pairs. How many more must he sell to earn the bonus?

$79.50
_____

3. On Monday, Tim sold 10 pairs of slippers. The slippers were $7.95 a pair. How much money did he take in on the sale of slippers?

$22.95
_____

4. Shoes were on sale for $7.50 off the regular price. Marie bought a pair of shoes on sale for $15.45. What was the regular price of the shoes?

$16.95
_____

5. Fanta spent $50.85 for 3 pairs of shoes. What was the average price of each pair she bought?

10 boxes
_____

6. Tim keeps the shoe boxes on shelves that are 65 inches long. Suppose a shoe box is 6.5 inches wide. How many boxes will fit on each shelf?

Super Sneaker Sale		
	Regular Price	Sale Price
High Flyers	$22.95	$11.50
Jumpers	$19.95	$ 9.98
Tennis Pros	$17.50	$ 8.75
Sport Line	$16.95	$ 8.50

$20.25
_____

7. Matt bought a pair of High Flyers and a pair of Tennis Pros during the Super Sneaker Sale. How much did he pay for the 2 pairs of shoes?

$8.45 more
_____

8. Phil bought 1 pair of Sport Line sneakers last week at the regular price. He bought another pair this week on sale. How much more did he pay for the sneakers last week?

$29.94
_____

9. Missy bought 3 pairs of Jumpers at the sale price. How much did she spend?

6½ hours
_____

10. Tim usually works $33\frac{1}{2}$ hours a week. To be a full-time employee, he must work 40 hours each week. How many more hours must he work each week to be a full-time employee?

Step Five: Check the Answer

(pages 10–11)

For each problem, use the two-part check to decide if the computed answer is a correct answer. If it is correct, write it again. If it is incorrect, cross through it and write the correct answer.

Musicland

3.1 km

4.5 km

6.2 km

city park

2.7 km

Pete's apartment

Sharon's house

1. Each Saturday, Sharon rides her bike from her house to Musicland for a piano lesson. After the lesson, she rides home the same way. How far does she ride in all to and from her lesson?

The Execution: 6.2
$\underline{\times\ 2}$
12.4

Computed Answer: 12.4 km

Correct Answer: _12.4 km_

2. Pete rides a bus from his apartment to Musicland for guitar lessons. After each lesson, he rides the bus to City Park. Then he takes another bus from the park to his apartment. How far does Pete ride on the bus?

The Execution: 4.5
3.1
$\underline{+\ 2.7}$
10.2

Computed Answer: ~~10.2 km~~

Correct Answer: _10.3 km_

3. How much farther does Sharon live from Musicland than Pete lives from Musicland?

The Execution: 6.2
$\underline{-\ 4.5}$
10.7

Computed Answer: ~~10.7 km~~

Correct Answer: _1.7 km_

4. Pete practiced the guitar for $3\frac{1}{2}$ hours last week. What was the average amount of time he practiced each day?

The Execution: $3\frac{1}{2} \div 7 = \frac{7}{2} \times \frac{1}{7} = \frac{1}{2}$

Computed Answer: $\frac{1}{2}$ hour

Correct Answer: _½ hour_

5. Sharon is playing 3 songs in a recital. The first song takes $2\frac{1}{2}$ minutes. The second song takes $1\frac{3}{4}$ minutes. The third song takes 3 minutes. How long will Sharon be playing the piano in the recital?

The Execution: $2\frac{1}{2} + 1\frac{3}{4} + 3 = 6\frac{4}{6} = 6\frac{2}{3}$

Computed Answer: ~~$6\frac{2}{3}$ min.~~

Correct Answer: _7¼ min._

6. Sharon has been taking piano lessons for $2\frac{1}{2}$ years. Pete has taken guitar lessons 3 times longer than Sharon has taken piano lessons. For how long has Pete been taking guitar lessons?

The Execution: $2\frac{1}{2} \times 3 = \frac{5}{2} \times \frac{3}{1} = \frac{15}{2} = 7\frac{1}{2}$

Computed Answer: $7\frac{1}{2}$ years

Correct Answer: _7½ years_

Cumulative Practice: Steps 1, 2, 3, 4, and 5
(pages 12–13)

Follow all five steps to solve each problem. Don't forget to check your answers. Make sure they are all reasonable *and* accurate.

3,939 people
_____

1. There were 2,643 adults and 1,296 children who attended a baseball game. How many people attended the game?

12 runs
_____

2. In the first game of the season, the home team had 13 hits and scored 7 runs. The visiting team had 15 hits and scored 5 runs. How many runs were scored in the first game?

88 points
_____

3. Anita bowled 3 games. Her total score for the 3 games was 264 points. What was her average score for each game?

24 min. 46 sec.
_____

4. Teena jogged once around the track in 6 minutes, 11.5 seconds. Suppose she continued to jog at this same pace. How long would it take her to go around the track 4 times?

4.4 seconds
_____

5. Carmen swam the 100-meter freestyle in 72.8 seconds. Margo swam the same distance in 77.2 seconds. How much faster was Carmen's time than Margo's time?

$3.25
_____

6. Paula spent $19.50 for 6 tickets to the hockey game. How much did each ticket cost?

69.23 seconds
_____

7. During a 400-meter relay, Gary ran the first leg in 16.25 seconds. Barry ran the second leg in 18.43 seconds. Terry ran the third leg in 19.21 seconds. Jerry ran the fourth leg in 15.34 seconds. How long did it take the relay team to run the whole race?

38 yards
_____

8. On the first play of the football game, Les rushed for $13\frac{1}{2}$ yards. On the second play, Mark caught a pass for a $24\frac{1}{2}$-yard gain. How many yards were gained in these two plays?

128 more yards
_____

9. During the game, the home team gained 98 yards rushing and 226 yards passing. How many more yards did they gain passing than rushing?

16,900 seats
_____

10. There are 33,800 seats in the ballpark. Suppose half of the seats are sold before game time. How many seats are left to be sold?

Too Much or Too Little Information

(pages 18–19)

If all the needed facts are given, solve the problem. If there is a missing fact, describe the fact you need.

1. Ann is in training for the swim team. Each day she does sit-ups and jogs $2\frac{3}{4}$ miles. How many sit-ups does she do in a week?

   Missing fact: Number of sit-ups Ann does each day

2. Pete does 15 sit-ups and 25 push-ups each day. Amir does twice as many sit-ups as Pete does. How many sit-ups does Amir do each day?

   30 sit-ups

3. Flora bought a sweater for $12.95 and a shirt that was on sale for $7.25 off the regular price. How much did she pay for the shirt?

   Missing fact: Regular price of the shirt

4. Jeff bought 3 belts that cost $5.49 each and 2 pairs of shoes that cost $19.95 each. How much did he spend on shoes?

   $39.90

5. Brad is 9 months old and weighs 18 pounds, 8 ounces. How much has he gained since birth?

   Missing fact: Brad's weight at birth

6. It took Kate 5 days to paint her house. The paint she used cost $24.95 a gallon. How much did Kate spend on paint for her house?

   Missing fact: Number of gallons of paint she used

7. There are 14,500 books in the local library. Most books may be checked out for 2 weeks. Reference books must be used in the library. How many books in the library may be checked out?

   Missing fact: Number of reference books in the library

8. On Monday, Jenny spent $1\frac{1}{4}$ hours doing math homework and $\frac{3}{4}$ of an hour doing science homework. On Tuesday, she spent $\frac{1}{2}$ an hour doing math homework and $1\frac{3}{4}$ hours writing a book report. How much longer did she spend on math homework on Monday than on Tuesday?

   ¾ of an hour

9. Tom's computer printer cost $875. It can print 10 lines in 15 seconds. Phil's printer cost $450. It can print the same number of lines in half the time. How long does it take Phil's printer to print 10 lines?

   7.5 seconds

Reading a Map

(pages 20–21)

Solve each problem. Use the map on page 20 for Problems 1–3.

271 miles
_____

1. Jean drove from Sacramento through Yosemite Village to Fresno. How many miles did she drive?

184 miles
_____

2. Assume a person wants to drive the shortest distance possible. How much farther is it from San Francisco to Crescent City than it is from San Francisco to Fresno?

1,512 miles
_____

3. Carl made 3 round trips from San Bernardino to Bishop. How many miles did he drive on these trips?

Use the map on page 21 for Problems 4–6.

470 miles
_____

4. Paul drove from Nashville through Knoxville and Asheville to Greensboro. How many miles did he drive in all?

2 miles
_____

5. How much farther is it from Charlotte to Asheville than from Knoxville to Chattanooga?

1,263 miles
_____

6. Three times a month, Chris drives from her home in Nashville to Chattanooga to Knoxville and back to Nashville. How many miles does she travel on these 3 trips?

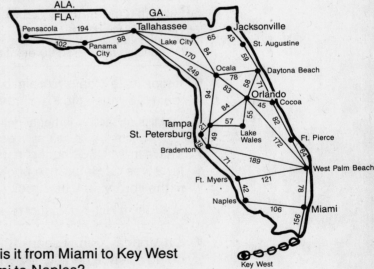

50 miles
_____

7. How much farther is it from Miami to Key West than it is from Miami to Naples?

41.5 miles
_____

8. Dee drove from St. Petersburg to Tallahassee in 6 hours. She traveled the same number of miles each hour. How far did she drive each hour?

430 miles
_____

9. Ken drives from Jacksonville to work in St. Augustine and back home again 5 days a week. How many miles does he drive to and from work each week?

Reading a Table

(pages 22–23)

Solve each problem. Use the table on page 22 for Problems 1–3.

42 minutes

1. Ruth rides the 6:15 A.M. train from Appleville to Oaksbury to work every day. How long is her ride to Oaksbury?

9:32 A.M.

2. Phil rides the 8:30 A.M. train from Cedarton to Oaksbury. Then he has a 15-minute walk to work. What time does Phil get to work?

45 minutes

3. Al rides the 6:45 P.M. train from work in Oaksbury to his home in Cedarton each day. How long is his train ride home?

Use the table on page 23 for Problems 4–6.

40 minutes

4. Parma caught the 1:05 P.M. bus at Englewood and rode to Osprey. How long was her bus ride?

1:52 P.M.

5. The 12:45 P.M. bus from North Port arrived at Sarasota Square Mall 3 minutes early. What time did the bus arrive at Sarasota Square Mall?

Sarasota Sq. Mall

6. Betty caught the bus at Venice Hospital at 4:00 P.M. She got off the bus 25 minutes later. Where did Betty get off the bus?

Airline Schedules

From: Atlanta, GA		To: New York, NY	From: New York, NY		To: Denver, CO
Departs	Arrives	Flight Number	Departs	Arrives	Flight Number
6:55 A.M.	9:00 A.M.	673	9:20 A.M.	11:50 A.M.	281
11:35 A.M.	1:40 P.M.	492	1:10 P.M.	3:20 P.M.	283
4:10 P.M.	6:20 P.M.	986	5:05 P.M.	7:15 P.M.	285
8:45 P.M.	10:50 P.M.	908			

2 hr. 10 min.

7. Mary took the 4:10 P.M. flight from Atlanta to New York. How long was her flight?

11:13 P.M.

8. The 8:45 P.M. flight from Atlanta to New York arrived 23 minutes late. What time did the flight arrive?

3:08 P.M.

9. Flight number 283 from New York to Denver arrived 12 minutes early. What time did the flight arrive?

20 minutes

10. How much longer is the 9:20 A.M. flight from New York to Denver than the 5:05 P.M. flight from New York to Denver?

Reading a Graph

(pages 24–25)

Solve each problem. Use the graph on page 24 for Problems 1–3.

7 degrees

1. In Boston, how many degrees warmer is the monthly normal temperature in August than in September?

12°F

2. One day in January, the temperature was 18 degrees below the normal for January. How low did the temperature go on that day?

17 degrees

3. One day in July, the high temperature was 91°F. How many degrees above the monthly normal for July was the temperature that day?

Use the graph on page 25 for Problems 4–6.

8 degrees

4. How many degrees warmer was the high temperature on Sunday than the low temperature on Sunday?

72°F

5. Forecasters are predicting that the low temperature on Saturday will be 5 degrees higher than the low temperature for Friday. What is the low temperature on Saturday predicted to be?

5 degrees

6. How many degrees cooler was the low temperature on Tuesday than the low temperature on Sunday?

SCIENCE PROJECT
Growth of Corn Plants

—— Plant A
watered every 2 days

—— Plant B
watered every 5 days

5 cm

7. How many centimeters did Plant A grow between the second and fourth weeks?

23 cm

8. Suppose Plant A grows 3 centimeters between the tenth and eleventh weeks. How tall will it be after the eleventh week?

9 cm

9. How many centimeters taller was Plant A than Plant B after 10 weeks?

4 cm

10. How many centimeters shorter was Plant B than Plant A after 4 weeks?

Using the Appendix
(pages 26–27)

Solve each problem. Refer to the Appendix if you need to.

676 weeks

1. Today is Chen's birthday. He is 13 years old. How many weeks old is Chen?

12.56 sq. ft.

2. A circular table top has a radius of 2 feet. What is the area of the table top? (Use 3.14 for π.)

1,792 mm²

3. The base of a triangular piece of tile is 56 millimeters. Its height is 64 millimeters. What is the area of the tile?

about 400 quarters

4. A quarter weighs about 5 grams. About how many quarters are in a bag that weighs 2 kilograms?

960 acres

5. A mall was built on $1\frac{1}{2}$ square miles of land. How many acres of land were used for the mall?

3.75 mm³

6. A box is 2.5 meters long, 1.5 meters wide, and 1 meter high. What is the volume of the box?

420,000 pounds

7. An empty airplane weighs about 150 tons. Suppose 60 tons of fuel and cargo are put on the plane. About how many pounds does the loaded plane weigh?

3 gallons

8. Jill is making orange juice. She has 8 cans of frozen juice. Each can is mixed with water to make $1\frac{1}{2}$ quarts of juice. How many gallons of juice will the 8 cans make?

26 feet

9. Sherrie wants to build a rectangular pen for her rabbit. The pen will be 9 feet long and 4 feet wide. How many feet of fencing does she need?

4 square yards

10. What will be the area of the rabbit pen in Problem 9 in square yards?

Choosing the Operation
(pages 28–29)

Solve each problem.

about 108 gallons

1. When you exercise, your heart pumps about 1.8 gallons of blood each minute. About how many gallons does your heart pump during 1 hour of exercise?

about 0.8 gallon

2. When you rest, your heart pumps about 48 gallons of blood in 1 hour. About how many gallons does your heart pump during each minute of rest?

2.5 times/sec.

3. After Rose jogged, her heart beat 150 times per minute. How many times per second did her heart beat?

90 times/min.

4. After Rose rested, her heart beat 1.5 times per second. How many times per minute did her heart beat?

1,140 breaths/hour

5. Luis breathes at a rate of 19 breaths per minute. How many breaths does Luis breathe in 1 hour?

50 grams more

6. In a healthy adult, the right lung weighs about 620 grams. The left lung weighs about 570 grams. How much more does the right lung weigh than the left lung?

5 cups

7. The daily amount of calcium in a diet should be 1.4 grams. One cup of whole milk contains 0.28 gram of calcium. How many cups of whole milk per day will supply the daily amount?

0.33 gram

8. One cup of milk contains 0.28 gram of calcium. Two slices of bread contain 0.04 gram of calcium. One slice of chicken contains 0.01 gram of calcium. Suppose you have a chicken sandwich and a cup of milk for lunch. How many grams of calcium will you eat?

3.1 mg more

9. One cup of carrots contains about 0.9 milligram of iron. One cup of spinach contains about 4 milligrams of iron. How much more iron is in a cup of spinach than is in a cup of carrots?

2 mg

10. One egg contains 1.4 milligrams of iron. A banana contains 0.6 milligram of iron. A bowl of cereal contains 0.8 milligram of iron. Mel ate an egg and a banana. How many milligrams of iron did she eat?

Two-Operation Problems

(pages 30–31)

Solve each problem. Use the calorie chart on page 30 if you need to.

330 calories
_____

1. To make a sandwich, Don used 2 slices of white bread and 2 slices of Swiss cheese. How many calories were in the sandwich?

67 calories more
_____

2. How many more calories are in $\frac{1}{2}$ grapefruit than in $\frac{1}{2}$ cantaloupe?

89 calories
_____

3. Beth used 1 banana, 1 apple, 1 peach, 1 cup of strawberries, and 1 cup of yogurt to make a fruit salad for 5 people. How many calories were in each serving?

100 calories more
_____

4. A loaf of bread contains 20 slices. How many more calories are there in a loaf of white bread than a loaf of whole wheat bread?

1,510 calories more
_____

5. Bud wants to eat no more than 2,800 calories per day. One day he ate a 565-calorie breakfast and a 725-calorie lunch. How many more calories could he eat that day and still stay within his goal?

750 calories
_____

6. To lose 1 pound of fat, a person must cut back about 3,000 calories. Suppose you want to lose 3 pounds in 12 days. How many calories will you have to cut back each day?

2,500 calories
_____

7. On Monday, Jim ate 2,200 calories. On Tuesday, he ate 2,750 calories. On Wednesday, he ate 2,550 calories. What was the average number of calories he ate per day during those 3 days?

27 calories more
_____

8. Marge had a blueberry muffin and an orange for breakfast. She had an apple and a cup of skim milk for a snack. How many more calories did she eat for breakfast than for the snack?

204 calories
_____

9. One gram of fat contains 9 calories. One gram of carbohydrate or protein contains 4 calories. How many total calories are in 12 grams of fat, 12 grams of carbohydrates, and 12 grams of protein?

50 calories more
_____

10. How many more calories are in 10 grams of fat than in 10 grams of protein? (Use the facts you need in Problem 9.)

Multiple-Step Problems

(pages 32–33)

Solve each problem.

$3.25
_____

1. Carlo bought 2 adult tickets and 3 children's tickets for the afternoon show. He gave the cashier at the ticket window $10. How much change did he get?

$5.00 more
_____

2. How much more does it cost to buy 2 adult tickets and 2 children's tickets to the evening show than to the afternoon show?

```
          TRI-CINEMA

afternoon shows — 2 P.M.
   adults      $2.25
   children     .75

evening shows — after 6 P.M.
   adults      $3.75
   children    1.75
```

$199.75 less
_____

3. For one afternoon show, Tri-Cinema sold 237 adult tickets and 356 children's tickets. How much less than $1,000 did the theater collect?

$407.00 more
_____

4. For one evening show, Tri-Cinema sold 315 adult tickets and 129 children's tickets. How much more than $1,000 did the theater collect?

670 people
_____

5. There are 3 movie theaters at Tri-Cinema. Theater I seats 50 fewer people than Theater II. Theater II seats twice as many people as Theater III. Theater III seats 360 people. How many people does Theater I seat?

1,000 empty seats
_____

6. For one show, Theater I sold 250 tickets. Theater II sold 310 tickets. Theater III sold 190 tickets. How many empty seats were left in all three theaters? (Use the facts you need in Problem 5.)

$3,100
_____

7. The theater owner has set aside $5,000 to replace one-half of the 360 seats in Theater III. The new seats will cost $45 each. How much more money will the owner need to set aside?

87 shows
_____

8. There are 5 shows in each of the 3 theaters on Saturday. There are 4 shows in each of the 3 theaters on Sunday through Friday. How many shows are there altogether in the 3 theaters during a week?

$.20
_____

9. At the snack bar, Matt bought 3 boxes of popcorn for $.85 each. He also bought 3 cups of grape juice for $.75 each. How much change did he get from $5.00?

3 adult, 1 children's
_____

10. Donna bought 4 tickets to an afternoon show. She gave the cashier $10 and got $2.50 in change. How many adult and how many children's tickets did she buy?

Checking Estimates and Computations
(pages 34–35)

Solve each problem. Show an estimated answer and a computed answer for each.

1. Plants Galore is having a sale. Maxine bought a hanging basket for $7.95 and a clay pot for $3.75. How much did she spend in all?

   Estimated Answer: $\dfrac{12}{(8 + 4 = 12)}$ Computed Answer: $\dfrac{\$11.70}{(7.95 + 3.75 = 11.70)}$

2. Beth has a $24.00 gift certificate from Plants Galore. How many lily plants for $3.95 each can she buy with her gift certificate?

   Estimated Answer: $\dfrac{6}{(24 \div 4 = 6)}$ Computed Answer: $\dfrac{6 \text{ plants}}{(24 \div 3.95 = 6.08 \text{ round down})}$

3. Joel works 38 hours a week at Plants Galore. He earns $4.95 per hour. How much does he earn in a week?

   Estimated Answer: $\dfrac{200}{(40 \times 5 = 200)}$ Computed Answer: $\dfrac{\$188.10}{(38 \times 4.95 = 188.10)}$

4. Plants Galore is open 50 hours a week. It is open 8 hours a day on Monday through Friday and 6 hours on Saturday. How many hours is it open on Sunday?

   Estimated Answer: $\dfrac{4}{(50 - (40 + 6) = 4)}$ Computed Answer: $\dfrac{4 \text{ hours}}{(8 \times 5 = 40;\ 40 + 6 = 46;\ 50 - 46 = 4)}$

5. Pete buys 3 ferns for $3.95 each and 12 cactus for $1.09 each. How much does he spend in all?

   Estimated Answer: $\dfrac{24}{[(3 \times 4) + (12 \times 1)] = 24}$ Computed Answer: $\dfrac{\$24.93}{[(3 \times 3.95) + (12 \times 1.09)] = \$24.93}$

6. Jake paid $8.29 for 6 ivy plants and a bag of soil. The soil cost $2.95. How much did each ivy plant cost?

   Estimated Answer: $\dfrac{0.83}{(8 - 3 = 5;\ 5 \div 6 = .83)}$ Computed Answer: $\dfrac{\$0.89}{(8.29 - 2.95 = 5.34;\ 5.34 \div 6 = .89)}$

7. Lara bought 3 plants for $1.79 each. How much change did she get from $10?

   Estimated Answer: $\dfrac{4}{(3 \times 2 = 6;\ 10 - 6 = 4)}$ Computed Answer: $\dfrac{\$4.63}{(3 \times 1.79 = 5.37;\ 10 - 5.37 = 4.63)}$

8. Rudy owes Plants Galore $49. He makes a $17 payment. He agrees to pay the rest in 4 weekly payments. How much will he pay each week?

   Estimated Answer: $\dfrac{7\frac{1}{2}}{(50 - 20 = 30;\ 30 \div 4 = 7\ 1/2)}$ Computed Answer: $\dfrac{\$8}{(49 - 17 = 32;\ 32 \div 4 = 8)}$

9. The owners of Plants Galore bought 50 hanging baskets for $4.95 each. They sold the baskets for $7.25 each. How much profit did they make on the sale of the 50 baskets?

   Estimated Answer: $\dfrac{100}{\substack{(50 \times 5 = 250;\ 50 \times 7 = 350;\\ 350 - 250 = 100)}}$ Computed Answer: $\dfrac{\$115}{\substack{(50 \times 4.95 = 247.50;\ 50 \times 7.25 =\\ 362.50;\ 362.50 - 247.50 = 115)}}$

Making a Diagram

(pages 40–41)

Solve each problem. Draw diagrams to help you.

165 cm

1. In a hamster cage, it is 65 cm from the exercise wheel to the food cup. A hamster gets off the wheel, walks 20 cm toward the food, turns around, and goes back to the wheel. Then it walks 30 cm toward the food, turns around, and goes back to the wheel. Finally, it walks straight from the wheel to the food cup. How far does the hamster walk in all?

8 combinations

2. Anne can play the piano and the flute. Barb can play the guitar and the drums. Carla can play the banjo and the violin. If each person plays one of her two instruments, how many combinations of three-instrument play are possible?

10 handshakes

3. There are 5 candidates running for class president. Before the election, each candidate shakes hands with all the other candidates. How many handshakes are there?

12 cups

4. For his science project, Marty is growing bean seeds in paper cups. He will test the following conditions—soil, food, and light. He will plant seeds in loam, sand, and clay. He will add plant food and he will not add plant food. He will place seeds in light and in shade. How many cups will he need to try all possible tests?

16 fence posts

5. Nikki is putting a fence around her rectangular garden. The garden is $16\frac{1}{2}$ feet by $27\frac{1}{2}$ feet. Nikki is spacing fence posts $5\frac{1}{2}$ feet apart. How many posts will she need?

12.6 km

6. Phil lives 3.5 kilometers from Burger Cafe. Central Park is 2.8 kilometers from Burger Cafe. Phil roller-skated from his house to Burger Cafe for lunch. He then skated to Central Park. On his way home, he stopped at Burger Cafe for water. Then he skated home. How far did Phil skate in all?

12th floor

7. Jean got into an elevator. She went down 6 floors, up 7 floors, and down 8 floors. She was then on the fifth floor. On what floor did Jean get on the elevator?

12 blocks

8. Tanya lives 3 blocks from Julie and $4\frac{1}{2}$ blocks from Debbie. Debbie's apartment is $1\frac{1}{2}$ blocks from Mort's Market. Tanya walked to Julie's house. Together the two girls walked back to Tanya's house. Then they walked to Debbie's apartment. The three girls then walked to Mort's Market. How far did Tanya walk in all?

4 times

9. A spider is climbing up a 12-foot pole. It climbs 3 feet at a time and then stops to rest. Each time it stops to rest, it slips back $\frac{1}{2}$ foot. The spider starts at the bottom of the pole. How many times will it stop to rest before it reaches the top of the pole?

11⅛ inches

10. Brad has 100 square tiles to make a square table top. Each tile is 1 inch on a side. Brad will leave $\frac{1}{8}$ inch between tiles when he makes the table top. How long will each side of the table top be?

Making a Line Graph

(pages 42–43)

Solve each problem. Make line graphs to help you.

__165 miles__

1. Heather's car can go 55 miles on 2 gallons of gas. How many miles will the car travel on 6 gallons of gas?

__8 gallons__

2. How many gallons of gas does Heather's car need to travel 220 miles?

__$28__

3. The cost to rent a bike at Rent-All is $7 for 2 days. How much will it cost to rent a bike for 8 days?

__12 days__

4. Bud has $42. For how many days may he rent a bike from Rent-All?

__10 A.M.__

5. Paul is driving to Rock City. He leaves at 7 A.M. and drives at a speed of 60 kilometers per hour. Paul's mother leaves from the same house and follows the same route to Rock City. She leaves at 8 A.M. and drives at 80 kilometers per hour. Paul has driven 180 kilometers. What time is it?

__160 km__

6. How far will Paul's mother have driven by 10 A.M.?

__11 A.M.__

7. At what time will Paul and his mother meet on the highway?

__24 meters__

8. A mother cat and her fastest kitten are running along the same street. The kitten starts 15 meters in front of its mother. The kitten runs at 5 meters per second. The mother cat runs at 8 meters per second. How far will the mother cat have gone in 3 seconds?

__4 seconds__

9. How long will it take the mother cat to go 32 meters?

__5 seconds__

10. How many seconds will it take the mother cat to catch her kitten?

Writing an Equation
(pages 44–45)

For each problem, write an equation and solve.

1. Mr. Lopez ordered 150 pairs of jogging shoes for his sports store. He received 85 pairs of shoes. How many more pairs of shoes does he need to complete his order?

   Equation: _____ $85 + n = 150$ _____   Answer: _____ 65 pairs _____

2. Vera and Jason work part-time at the sports store. Last week, Vera worked 20 hours. This is $2\frac{1}{2}$ times the number of hours Jason worked. How many hours did Jason work?

   Equation: _____ $2\frac{1}{2} \times n = 20$ _____   Answer: _____ 8 hours _____

3. Marge spends $14.94 for 6 pairs of socks. How much does each pair of socks cost?

   Equation: _____ $14.94 \div 6 = n$ _____   Answer: _____ $2.49 _____

4. Beth has saved $36.00 to buy a new tennis racket. This is $\frac{2}{3}$ of what she needs to buy the racket. How much does the new racket cost?

   Equation: _____ $\frac{2}{3} \times n = 36$ _____   Answer: _____ $54 _____

5. Soccer balls are on sale for $13.45. This is $4.50 off the regular price. What is the regular price?

   Equation: _____ $13.45 + 4.50 = n$ _____   Answer: _____ $17.95 _____

6. Steve spent $69.44 for 2 pairs of knee pads and a skateboard. The knee pads cost $4.95 a pair. How much did the skateboard cost?

   Equation: _____ $(2 \times 4.95) + n = 69.44$ _____   Answer: _____ $59.54 _____

7. Mr. Lopez ordered 4 times as many baseballs as bats for his store. He ordered 180 baseballs. How many bats did he order?

   Equation: _____ $4 \times n = 180$ _____   Answer: _____ 45 bats _____

8. Softballs cost $.75 more than baseballs. The softballs cost $4.95 each. How much do baseballs cost?

   Equation: _____ $n + .75 = 4.95$ _____   Answer: _____ $4.20 _____

9. Maria bought 3 cans of tennis balls and a visor for $13.89. The tennis balls cost $2.98 a can. How much did the visor cost?

   Equation: _____ $(3 \times 2.98) + n = 13.89$ _____   Answer: _____ $4.95 _____

Using a Formula

(pages 46–47)

Use the formulas listed on page 46 or in the Appendix on page 121 to help you solve these problems.

2,465 miles
_____

1. A plane flew at an average speed of 580 mph from Los Angeles to New York in $4\frac{1}{4}$ hours. How far did the airplane fly?

48 mph
_____

2. A bus traveled 120 miles from New York to Hartford in $2\frac{1}{2}$ hours. What was the average rate of speed the bus traveled?

10:30 A.M.
_____

3. Robyn began jogging at 9 A.M. She jogged at a rate of 4 miles per hour for 6 miles. What time did she stop jogging?

$675
_____

4. Corey invested $2,500 at 6% simple interest for $4\frac{1}{2}$ years. How much interest did he earn?

2 years
_____

5. Fran borrowed $750 at 11.5% simple interest. For how long did she borrow the money if the interest she paid was $172.50?

$7\frac{1}{2}$%
_____

6. Chris invested $1,200 at simple interest. After 3 years, she had earned $270. What was the interest rate?

$5,000
_____

7. John borrowed some money from a bank for 5 years at a simple interest rate of 12.5%. He paid $3,125 in interest for the 5 years. How much money did John borrow?

12.56 sq. ft.
_____

8. A circular table top has a diameter of 4 feet. What is the area of the table top?

12 feet
_____

9. The area of a rectangular rug is 108 square feet. The rug is 9 feet wide. How long is the rug?

4 feet
_____

10. The volume of a shipping carton is 24 cubic feet. The carton is 2 feet wide and 3 feet long. How high is the carton?

Solving a Simpler Problem

(pages 48–49)

Solve each problem by thinking of a similar but simpler problem.

28 ways

1. How many ways can you add 3 numbers to get a sum of 6? (Here are three ways: 6 + 0 + 0, 5 + 0 + 1, 5 + 1 + 0.)

91 ways

2. How many ways can you add 3 numbers to get a sum of 12?

56 ways

3. How many ways can you add 4 numbers to get a sum of 5?

26 triangles

4. How many triangles are in this figure?

66 roads

5. Suppose 1 road is built to connect a single pair of cities. (Each road can connect only 2 cities.) What is the largest number of roads that could be built to connect 12 cities?

13 squares

6. How many squares are in this figure?

8 A.M.

7. Nikki and Lori live 152 kilometers apart. They plan to leave their homes at the same time and ride toward each other. Nikki will ride at 16 kilometers per hour. Lori will ride at 22 kilometers per hour. At what time must they leave their homes in order to meet for lunch exactly at noon?

24 triangles

8. How many triangles are in this figure?

729 members

9. Benny is starting a computer club. He is the only member now. He plans to have each member bring in 2 new members each month. Suppose his plan works. How many members will the club have at the end of 6 months?

78 angles

10. How many angles are in this figure? (AOB, AOC, and BOL are 3 angles.)

Using Ratio Proportions

(pages 50–51)

Write a proportion for each problem. Then solve. Use the scale drawing on page 50 for Problems 1–3.

<u>3 meters by 3.75 meters</u>

1. What are the actual dimensions (length and width) of the smaller bedroom in Beth's apartment?
$\frac{2}{3} = \frac{2}{n}$ $n = 3$ $\frac{2}{3} = \frac{2.5}{n}$ $n = 3.75$

<u>11.25 meters by 6.75 meters</u>

2. What are the actual outside dimensions of Beth's apartment?
$\frac{2}{3} = \frac{7.5}{n}$ $n = 11.25$ $\frac{2}{3} = \frac{4.5}{n}$ $n = 6.75$

<u>3 centimeters</u>

3. Beth is going to add a patio that is 4.5 meters wide. She will use the same scale used for the apartment. How wide will the patio be in her scale drawing?
$\frac{2}{3} = \frac{n}{4.5}$ $n = 3$

<u>16 inches</u>

4. A 747 jet airliner is about 225 feet long. It has a wingspan of about 200 feet. A scale model of the plane is 18 inches long. What is the wingspan of the model?
$\frac{18}{225} = \frac{n}{200}$ $n = 16$

<u>528 inches (or 44 feet)</u>

5. A scale model of a steam locomotive is 11 inches long. The ratio of the model to the actual train is 1 to 48. What is the length of the actual locomotive?
$\frac{1}{48} = \frac{11}{n}$ $n = 528$

<u>2,700 miles</u>

6. An airplane travels 1,800 miles in 4 hours. At this rate, how far will it go in 6 hours?
$\frac{1,800}{4} = \frac{n}{6}$ $n = 2,700$

<u>18 students</u>

7. The ratio of students with blue eyes to students with brown eyes is 3 to 2. Twelve students have brown eyes. How many students have blue eyes?
$\frac{3}{n} = \frac{2}{12}$ $n = 18$

<u>16 pages</u>

8. Al can type 2 pages in 15 minutes. How many pages can he type in 3 hours?
$\frac{2}{15} = \frac{n}{120}$ $n = 16$

<u>18 strikeouts</u>

9. Joan is a softball pitcher. She strikes out 3 of every 7 batters she faces. Suppose she faces 42 batters. How many strikeouts does she have?
$\frac{3}{n} = \frac{7}{42}$ $n = 18$

<u>6 hours</u>

10. Carlos read 25 pages in 45 minutes. How many hours will it take him to read 200 pages?
$\frac{25}{45} = \frac{200}{n}$ $n = 360$

Using Logical Reasoning

(pages 52–53)

Use logical reasoning to solve each problem.

trumpet
_____

1. Rosa, Stan, and Tom each play a different instrument. They play a flute, a guitar, and a trumpet.
   Clue 1: Stan and the trumpet player walk to school together.
   Clue 2: Tom loves to sing while his friend plays the guitar.
   Clue 3: Rosa will play the flute in a concert next week.
   What instrument does Tom play?

Marcy
_____

2. Marcy, Thad, Carlotta, and Jake each enjoy playing a different sport. They play baseball, basketball, football, and volleyball. One of Marcy's friends in the group plays basketball. Carlotta and Jake do not play volleyball. Thad enjoys playing football. Jake used to like playing baseball but has changed his favorite. Who plays volleyball?

Jim
_____

3. Tim, Jim, Kim, and Sim ran a race. At the end of the race, Tim was 20 yards behind Jim. Jim was 50 yards ahead of Kim. Sim was 30 yards ahead of Kim. Who won the race?

4. You have 20 coins to arrange in 4 stacks. All the stacks have an even number of coins. The second stack has twice as many coins as the fourth stack. Each stack has a different number of coins. Each stack has a least 1 coin. The third stack has the most coins. How many coins are in each stack?

   1st stack ___6___; 2nd stack ___4___; 3rd stack ___8___; 4th stack ___2___

5. A rowboat can carry only 175 pounds. Jean weighs 125 pounds. Joan weighs 100 pounds. Jan weighs 75 pounds. Jean, Joan, and Jan are together on one side of a lake. How may they use the rowboat to cross the lake?

   Joan and Jan cross the lake. Joan (or Jan) returns. Jean crosses the lake. Jan
   _____
   (or Joan) returns. Joan and Jan cross the lake.
   _____

6. Suppose you have a 3-quart pail and an 8-quart pail. There are no markings on either pail. How may you use these pails to get exactly 4 quarts of water in the larger pail?

   Answers may vary. One possibility: Fill 3-quart pail 3 times, pouring into 8-quar
   _____
   pail each time. On third pour, 1 quart will be left in 3-quart pail. Empty water
   _____
   from 8-quart pail. Put 1 quart of water in 8-quart pail. Fill 3-quart pail. Pour into
   _____
   8-quart pail.
   _____

Exact or Estimated Answers

(pages 54–55)

For each problem, first decide whether an exact or an estimated answer is necessary. Then solve the problem.

no
(estimated)

1. Denise has a 312-page book to read in 6 days. Suppose she reads 45 pages each day. Will she finish the book in 6 days?

about 700,000 more people (estimated) (or about 680,000 more people— depends on rounding)

2. The population of Phoenix, Arizona, increased from 106,818 in 1950 to 789,704 in 1980. About how many more people lived in Phoenix in 1980 than in 1950?

$14.24
(exact)

3. Mavis bought 3 books that cost $4.98, $5.29, and $3.29. The clerk added $0.68 tax. Mavis paid for the books with a check. For how much was the check?

yes
(estimated)

4. Brad has a part-time job. He has saved $85 to buy a new stereo and head-phones. The stereo costs $59.95. The headphones cost $18.99. Has Brad saved enough money?

about 25,000 books
(estimated)

5. Each shelf in the library has about 25 books. There are 1,197 shelves of books in the library. About how many books are in the library?

$3.06
(exact)

6. Mark bought 3 pounds of tomatoes for $0.79 per pound and 1 head of let-tuce for $0.69. He gave the clerk the correct amount of money. How much did he give the clerk?

more than 20 hours
(estimated)

7. Claire works at least 20 hours each week. Last week, she worked $4\frac{1}{2}$ hours each on Monday, Wednesday, and Friday. She worked $5\frac{1}{2}$ hours each on Tuesday and Thursday. Did Claire work more than or less than 20 hours last week?

about 80 blocks
(estimated)

8. Jenny walks $8\frac{1}{4}$ blocks each way to and from school each day. About how many blocks does she walk during a 5-day school week?

7.1 milligrams more
(exact)

9. Pete needs 18 milligrams of iron in his diet each day. He had 4.6 milli-grams for breakfast and 6.3 milligrams for lunch. How many more milli-grams does he need?

yes
(estimated)

10. Lou has $23\frac{1}{2}$ yards of fabric to make covers for furniture. He needs $16\frac{1}{4}$ yards for a sofa, $3\frac{1}{2}$ yards for a chair, and $1\frac{3}{4}$ yards for a stool. Does Lou have enough fabric?

More Than One Strategy

(pages 56–57)

Teacher Note: The most likely strategy is shown for your information. Students may choose other strategies.

Use whatever strategy works best for you to solve each problem.

$16.65
_____
(proportion)

1. Books are sale priced at 3 for $9.99. At that rate, how much will 5 books cost?

about 12:30 P.M.
_____
(line graph)

2. Nancy left Hometown at 9 A.M. She drove at an average speed of 25 miles per hour. Jill followed her 1 hour later, driving at an average speed of 35 miles per hour. About what time did Jill overtake Nancy?

$12,000
_____
(equation)

3. A piece of land costs $30,000. That is $2\frac{1}{2}$ times as much as it cost in 1980. How much did the land cost in 1980?

15 games
_____
(diagram)

4. Six students played in the chess tournament. Each student played every other student once. How many games were played?

135 miles
_____
(equation)

5. A bus is traveling at an average speed of 45 miles per hour. How far will it travel in 3 hours?

36 choices
_____
(diagram)

6. Burger Cafe sells 6 kinds of burgers with a choice of 3 sauces and a choice of 2 kinds of rolls. How many choices are there for a burger with sauce on a roll?

$97.50
_____
(formula)

7. Mel invested $750 at $6\frac{1}{2}$% simple interest for 2 years. How much interest did she earn?

3 inches
_____
(proportion)

8. A map is drawn with a scale of 2 inches = 30 miles. Suppose an actual road is 45 miles long. How long will the road be on the map?

9. Al, Barb, Cal, and Dee swam a relay. At the end of the race,
   Dee was 2 yards ahead of Al.
   Al was 1 yard behind Barb.
   Barb was 3 yards ahead of Cal.
   In what order did the four finish the race?

   1st place __Dee__ ; 2nd place __Barb__ ; 3rd place __Al__ ; 4th place __Cal__
   (diagram)

3¼ hours
_____
(equation)

10. Rose spent $5\frac{1}{2}$ hours working on her science project. This is $2\frac{1}{4}$ hours more than Teena spent on her science project. How long did Teena spend on her project?

Checking Accounts

(pages 62–63)

Answer these questions about checks and check registers.

$78.90

1. Sherry has $114.69 in her checking account. She writes a check to Green Thumb Nursery for $35.79. How much money does Sherry have left in her checking account?

$182.88

2. Joel has $57.13 in his checking account. He deposited $125.75. How much money does he have in his checking account now?

This is Pam's check register.

NUMBER	DATE	DESCRIPTION OF TRANSACTION	PAYMENT/DEBIT (–)		DEPOSIT/CREDIT (+)		BALANCE	
						$	328	69
204	4/12	The Food Mart	$ 13	50	$		315	19
	4/15	Deposit			125	50	440	69
205	4/16	Beeline Buslines	63	95			376	74
206	4/18	General Telephone	24	69			352	05
207	4/30	The Music Shop	13	95			338	10
	5/2	Deposit			25	13	363	23

3. What was Pam's balance after she made the deposit on April 15? Write the new balance on the register.

4. What was the balance after Pam wrote check number 205? Write the new balance on the register.

5. What was Pam's balance after her check to General Telephone? Write the new balance on the register.

6. On April 30, Pam wrote check number 207 to The Music Shop for $13.95. Complete the register for this check.

7. On May 2, Pam made a deposit of $25.13 into her checking account. Complete the register for this deposit.

8. Bob wrote a check for $20.89 on April 3, 1987. He made the check out to SportLine to pay for a new soccer ball and knee pads. Complete Bob's check.

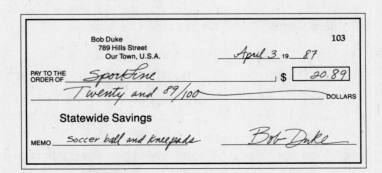

Bob Duke
789 Hills Street
Our Town, U.S.A.   103

April 3 19 87

PAY TO THE
ORDER OF   SportLine $ 20.89

Twenty and 89/100   DOLLARS

Statewide Savings

MEMO   Soccer ball and kneepads   Bob Duke

Unit Pricing

(pages 64–65)

For Problems 1–5, find the unit price to the nearest cent.

1. 3 grapefruit for $0.89: ___$0.30/grapefruit___

2. 3 pounds of potatoes for $1.29: ___$0.43/lb.___

3. 4-pack of light bulbs for $2.19: ___$0.55/bulb___

4. 16-ounce can of peanuts for $2.69: ___$0.17/oz.___

5. 1 dozen eggs for $0.89: ___$0.07/egg___

For Problems 6–11, find the unit prices. Then tell which item is the better buy.

6. 3-lb. bag of apples for $1.89 *or* a 5-lb. bag of apples for $3.25

   Better Buy: ___3-lb. bag of apples___
   (3-lb. bag = $0.63/lb.; 5-lb. bag = $0.65/lb.)

7. package of 8 corn muffins for $1.59 *or* package of 12 corn muffins for $1.99

   Better Buy: ___12 corn muffins___
   (8-pack = $0.20/muffin; 12-pack = $0.17/muffin)

8. 8-oz. bottle of salad dressing for $1.09 *or* 20-oz. bottle of salad dressing for $2.39

   Better Buy: ___20-oz. bottle of dressing___
   (8-oz. bottle = $0.14/oz.; 20-oz. bottle = $0.12/oz.)

9. 9-oz. box of rice for $1.29 *or* 13-oz. box of rice for $2.08

   Better Buy: ___9-oz. box of rice___
   (9-oz. box = $0.14/oz.; 13-oz. box = $0.16/oz.)

10. 6 oranges for $0.79 *or* 8 oranges for $0.95

    Better Buy: ___8 oranges for $0.95___
    (6 oranges = $0.13/orange; 8 oranges = $0.12/orange)

11. 11-oz. box of cereal for $1.69 *or* 15-oz. box of cereal for $2.12

    Better Buy: ___15-oz. box of cereal___
    (11-oz. box = $0.15/oz.; 15-oz. box = $0.14/oz.)

For Problems 12–14, answer the question.

$2.40 (3 cans = $0.23/can; 8 cans = $0.20/can)

12. Three cans of LiteLine juice sell for $0.69. Eight cans of Zippy juice sell for $1.60. You buy 12 cans of the better buy. How much do you spend?

$1.92 (16-oz. loaf = $0.04/oz.; 20-oz. loaf = $0.05/oz.)

13. A 16-oz. loaf of All-Grain Bread sells for $0.64. A 20-oz. loaf of Natural Bread sells for $1.00. You buy 3 loaves of the better buy. How much do you spend?

$6.20 (1-lb. cheese = $2.48/lb.; 1½-lb. cheese = $2.58/lb.)

14. One pound of DairyLine Swiss cheese costs $2.48. One and one-half pounds of Best Buy Swiss cheese cost $3.87. You buy 2.5 pounds of the better buy. How much do you spend?

Recipes

(pages 66–67)

Solve each problem. Use the recipe on page 66 for Problems 1–3.

1⅛ pounds

1. How much ground beef is needed to make a meat loaf for 3 people?

1⅞ cups

2. How much milk is needed to make a meat loaf for 6 people?

1½ teaspoons

3. How much pepper is needed to make a meat loaf for 12 people?

Use the recipe on page 67 for Problems 4–7.

3 eggs

4. How many eggs are needed to make 27 banana oatmeal muffins?

¼ cup

5. How much cooking oil is needed to make 9 muffins?

1½ cups

6. How much honey is needed to make 36 muffins?

⅔ cup

7. What amount of oats is needed to make 12 muffins?

Use this recipe for Problems 8–12.

Glazed Carrots

2 cups cooked, sliced carrots   1 tablespoon lemon juice
4 tablespoons margarine   1 teaspoon chopped parsley
1½ teaspoons brown sugar

Melt margarine in pan. Add sugar and lemon juice. Mix well.
Stir in carrots. Shake pan to glaze carrots. Place in serving
bowl and garnish with parsley.   Serves 6

---

3 cups

8. What amount of carrots is needed to prepare glazed carrots for 9 people?

2 tablespoons

9. How much margarine is needed to prepare glazed carrots for 3 people?

3 teaspoons

10. How much brown sugar is needed to prepare glazed carrots for 12 people?

½ tablespoon

11. How much lemon juice is needed to prepare glazed carrots for 3 people?

15 people

12. How many people may be served from a recipe using 5 cups of sliced carrots?

Budgets

(pages 68–69)

Answer each question. Use the circle graph on page 68 for Problems 1–3.

$8.20

1. Suppose Gina earns $82. How much may she spend on recreation?

No, she did not.

2. Last week Gina worked 5 days and earned $88. It cost Gina $1.25 each way to ride the bus to and from her part-time job. Did Gina stay within her budget for transportation last week?

$43.50

3. One week Gina earned $78. The next week she earned $96. How much did she save for the two weeks?

Use the circle graph on page 69 for Problems 4–6. The Simons used the same plan to budget their money last year when their combined take-home pay was $32,500.

$6,500

4. How much money did the Simons budget for food last year?

$8,125

5. How much money did the Simons budget for clothing and transportation together last year?

$3,250 more

6. How much more money did the Simons budget for housing than for food?

Pablo has a part-time job at the Bike Shop. This circle graph shows how he budgets the money he earns.

Pablo's Budget

$28.50

7. One week Pablo earned $95. How much did he save?

$4.40

8. Suppose Pablo earns $88. How much more may he spend on clothing than on food?

Yes, he can buy the radio.

9. Last week Pablo earned $83. This week he earned $72. He wants to buy his brother a radio that costs $12.95. Suppose he used the money budgeted for gifts last week and this week. Can he buy the radio?

No, he cannot buy the jacket.

10. This month Pablo has earned $338. He used money budgeted for clothing to buy a jacket for $29.95. He wants to buy a warm-up suit for $39.95. Can he buy the warm-up suit and stay within his budget for this month?

Probability

(pages 70–71)

Solve these probability problems. Use the spinner on page 70 for Problems 1–3.

2/6 or 1/3

1. What is the probability of spinning a 1 or a 2?

0/6 or 0

2. What is the probability of spinning an 8?

6/6 or 1

3. What is the probability of spinning a number less than 8?

F	A	V	O	R	A	B	L	E

These letter cards are placed in a bag. Each card is made of the same material. Each card is shaped exactly the same. One card is picked without looking. Answer Problems 4–7 about the letter cards.

1/9

4. What is the probability of picking a V?

2/9

5. What is the probability of picking an A?

4/9

6. What is the probability of picking a vowel?

5/9

7. What is the probability of picking a consonant?

There are 8 green blocks, 6 yellow blocks, 4 red blocks, and 2 white blocks in a bag. They are all the same except in color. Imagine picking a block without looking. Answer Problems 8–10 about the blocks.

8/20 or 2/5

8. What is the probability of picking a green block?

10/20 or 1/2

9. What is the probability of picking a yellow block or a red block?

0/20 or 0

10. What is the probability of picking a purple block?

2/8 or 1/4

11. There a 6 red socks and 2 blue socks in a drawer. Imagine picking 1 sock without looking. What is the probability that the sock will be blue?

2/6 or 1/3

12. These numbers are placed on the faces of a number cube: 1, 2, 2, 3, 3, 3. What is the probability that 2 lands up when the cube is tossed?

Sales Tax

(pages 72–73)

Solve each problem. Read the questions carefully! Sometimes, you will need to find the amount of sales tax. Other times, you will need to find the total cost.

$1.50
_____

1. The price of a bracelet is $24.95. The sales tax is 6%. Find the amount of tax.

$2.74
_____

2. The price of a lamp is $54.75. The sales tax is 5%. Find the amount of tax.

$13.50
_____

3. The price of a suitcase is $180. The sales tax is $7\frac{1}{2}$%. Find the amount of tax.

$14.21
_____

4. The price of a camera is $154. A lens kit is $49. The sales tax is 7%. You buy the camera and lens kit. Find the amount of tax you pay.

$0.48
_____

5. The price of a pair of socks is $1.99. The sales tax is 4%. You buy 6 pairs of socks. Find the amount of tax you pay.

$73.49
_____

6. The price of a guitar is $69.99. The sales tax is 5%. Find the total cost.

$200.87
_____

7. The price of a sewing machine is $189.50. The sales tax is 6%. Find the total cost.

$53.24
_____

8. The price of a sleeping bag is $49.99. The sales tax is $6\frac{1}{2}$%. Find the total cost.

$175.45
_____

9. The price of a table-tennis table is $139.98. A set of paddles, balls, and net is $23.99. The sales tax is 7%. Find the total cost.

$84
_____

10. The price of a black-and-white TV is $79.99. A color TV is $159.99. The sales tax is 5%. How much more would you pay for the color TV than for the black-and-white TV?

$10.56
_____

11. The price of a can of tennis balls is $2.49. The sales tax is 6%. Find the total cost of 4 cans of tennis balls.

$310.30
_____

12. The price of a table is $150. Chairs are $35 each. The sales tax is 7%. Find the total cost of a table and 4 chairs.

Discounts

(pages 74–75)

Solve each problem. Read the question carefully.

$17.40
_____

1. A 3-speed bike originally sold for $115.99. This week the store is giving a 15% discount off the original price. What is the discount?

$12.50
_____

2. Roller skates usually sell for $49.99. The store is having a 25% close-out sale. How much will the discount be during the close-out sale?

$15.99
_____

3. Clock radios usually sell for $19.99 each. They are on sale for 20% off the original price. Find the sale price of a radio.

$467.48
_____

4. A home computer sells for $299.99. A color monitor sells for $249.99. A 15% discount is given to people who buy both the computer and the monitor. How much is the computer and monitor?

$94.40 more
_____

5. A manual typewriter usually sells for $76.99. An electric typewriter usually sells for $194.99. A 20% discount is given on each typewriter this week. How much more does the electric typewriter cost than the manual typewriter this week?

20%
_____

6. Warm-up suits are on sale for $10 off the original price of $50. What is the percent of discount? (Hint: Look at Example B on page 74.)

25%
_____

7. Boots are on sale for $12.50 off the original price of $50. What is the percent of discount?

$200.00
_____

8. During a 15%-off sale, the discount on a camera was $30. What was the original price of the camera?

40%
_____

9. A telescope is on sale for $75. The original price was $125. What is the percent of discount? (Hint: First find the amount of discount.)

20%
_____

10. A microscope is on sale for $39.99. The original price was $49.99. What is the percent of discount?

Time Cards
(pages 76–77)

Answer the questions. Use the time card on page 76 for Problems 1–4.

$8.85

1. Next month, Clay will get a raise. He will earn $5.90 per hour. He will receive time and a half for overtime. How much will Clay be paid per hour of overtime?

$280.25

2. The week after his raise, Clay worked the same number of hours he worked during the week ending April 30. He was paid time and a half for the time over 40 hours he worked. How much did he earn during the first week after his raise?

$17.70

3. One week after his raise, Clay worked 36 hours. The next week he worked 39 hours. How much more did he earn during the week he worked 39 hours?

$32.45

4. The following week Clay worked 43 hours. How much more did he earn the week he worked 43 hours than the week he worked 39 hours?

Use the following time card to answer Problems 5–8.

Party Shop

Name _Jean Brown_

Week Ending _July 31_

	IN	OUT		IN	OUT	HOURS WORKED
Mon.	9:00	12:00	L	1:00	5:00	7
Tues.	9:00	1:30	U	2:00	5:30	8
Wed.	10:00	2:00	N	2:30	6:00	7½
Thurs.	9:00	12:30	C	1:30	7:00	9
Fri.	9:00	2:00	H			5
Sat.				12:00	6:00	6
					Total Hours	42½

5. Complete the "HOURS WORKED" column on the time card for Jean Brown.

$54

6. Jean is paid $7.20 an hour. How much did Jean earn on Wednesday?

$10.80

7. Jean is paid time and a half for the time over 40 hours that she works. How much is she paid per hour of overtime?

$315

8. How much did Jean earn during the week ending July 31?

$335.75

9. Vern earns $8.50 per hour. She earns time and a half if she works more than 35 hours a week. Vern worked 38 hours last week. How much did she earn?

34 hours

10. This week Vern earned $289. How many hours did she work?

Sampling
(pages 78–79)

Answer these questions. Use the sample chart on page 78 for Problems 1–3.

20%
_____

178 students
_____

30%
_____

1. What percent of students in the sample like jazz music best?

2. There are 890 students in the school. Based on the sample, how many students in the school like jazz music best?

3. What percent of the students in the sample like country _or_ jazz music best?

There are 1,250 students at Murphy School. The school newspaper reporter asked 50 students to name their favorite type of fiction. The results are shown in the chart.

Murphy School

Favorite Type of Fiction

Adventure	ЖЖ ЖЖ //	12
Mystery	ЖЖ ЖЖ	10
Historical Novel	ЖЖ ///	8
Romance	ЖЖ //	7
Horror	ЖЖ	5
Science Fiction	ЖЖ ///	8

20%
_____

250 students
_____

40%
_____

500 students
_____

50 more students
_____

1,800 customers
_____

300 listeners
_____

4. What percent of students in the sample like mystery stories best?

5. Based on this sample, how many students in the school like mystery stories best?

6. What percent of students in the sample like adventure stories _or_ science fiction best?

7. Based on this sample, how many students in the school like adventure stories _or_ science fiction best?

8. Based on this sample, how many more students in the school like romance than horror stories?

9. There was a random sample of 50 customers at a grocery store. Twenty said they ate fish at least once a week. Based on this sample, how many of the 4,500 customers who shopped that day eat fish at least once a week?

10. There was a random sample of 100 radio listeners. Thirty people said they would rather listen to talk shows than to music. Now suppose 1,000 radio listeners are sampled. Based on the earlier sample, how many will rather listen to talk shows than to music?

Whole-Book Review

Teacher Note: Accept variations in students' plans as long as the plans yield correct answers.

Read and reread each word problem. Then follow the directions to show your solution to the problem.

1. Sports World is having a one-day sale on skateboards. All skateboards are on sale for (30% off) the original price. During the sale, Phil bought a skateboard that originally sold for ($49) <u>What was the sale price of the skateboard?</u>

   a. Underline the question.
   b. Circle the needed facts in the problem.

   c. Describe your plan: <u>Find the sale price. (discount = rate of discount × original price; sale price = original price − discount)</u>

   d. If an estimate can be made, show it here: <u>.3 × 50 = 15; 50 − 15 = 35</u>

   e. Carry out your plan. Answer: <u>$34.30   (.30 × 49 = 14.70; 49 − 14.70 = 34.30)</u>

   f. Check your answer. If you got an incorrect answer, tell how you know it is wrong. Then write the correct answer.

   <u>Students who got incorrect answers should mention computation error or</u>

   <u>that the answer was not reasonable.</u>

2. <u>How many degrees warmer was the high temperature on Wednesday than the high temperature on Sunday?</u>

   a. Underline the question.
   b. Circle the needed facts in the problem.

Daily High Temperature

Temperature (°F) / Days: S M T W Th F S

   c. Describe your plan: <u>Read the graph and subtract Sunday's high from Wednesday's high.</u>

   d. If an estimate can be made, show it here: <u>cannot be made</u>

   e. Carry out your plan. Answer: <u>16 degrees warmer   (80 − 64 = 16)</u>

   f. Check your answer. If you got an incorrect answer, tell how you know it is wrong. Then write the correct answer.

   <u>Students who got incorrect answers should mention computation error or</u>

   <u>that the answer was not reasonable.</u>

3. Pat bought (16 yards) of fabric to re-cover her sofa. This is $(9\frac{1}{2}$ yards more) than she bought to re-cover her chair. How much fabric did Pat buy to re-cover her chair?

a. Underline the question.

b. Circle the needed facts in the problem.

c. Describe your plan: ___Write an equation. (n + 9½ = 16)___

d. If an estimate can be made, show it here: ___cannot be made___

e. Carry out your plan. Answer: ___6½ yards___   (n = 16 − 9½; n = 6½)

f. Check your answer. If you got an incorrect answer, tell how you know it is wrong. Then write the correct answer.

Students who got incorrect answers should mention computation error or that the answer was not reasonable.

4. Anne had ($389.15) in her checking account. She wrote a check to Mort's Market for ($23.10.) How much money does Anne have left in her checking account?

a. Underline the question.

b. Circle the needed facts in the problem.

c. Describe your plan: ___Find the balance by subtracting the amount on the check from the former balance.___

d. If an estimate can be made, show it here: ___400 − 20 = 380___

e. Carry out your plan. Answer: ___$366.05___   (389.15 − 23.10 = 366.05)

f. Check your answer. If you got an incorrect answer, tell how you know it is wrong. Then write the correct answer.

Students who got incorrect answers should mention computation error or that the answer was not reasonable.

5. Ruth can type (3 pages) in (20 minutes.) How many pages can Ruth type in 1 hour?

   a. Underline the question.

   b. Circle the needed facts in the problem.

   c. Describe your plan: _____ Write a proportion. ($\frac{3}{n} = \frac{20}{60}$) _____

   _____

   d. If an estimate can be made, show it here: _____ cannot be made _____

   e. Carry out your plan. Answer: _____ 9 pages _____ ($20n = 180; n = 9$)

   f. Check your answer. If you got an incorrect answer, tell how you know it is wrong. Then write the correct answer.

      Students who got incorrect answers should mention computation error or

      that the answer was not reasonable.

Snyders' Budget

6. The graph shows how the Snyders plan to budget their money. Their take-home pay last month totaled ($1,800.) How much should they have put away for savings?

   a. Underline the question.

   b. Circle the needed facts in the problem.

   c. Describe your plan: _____ Find 15% of $1,800. _____

   _____

   d. If an estimate can be made, show it here: _____ $.10 \times 2,000 = 200$ _____

   e. Carry out your plan. Answer: _____ $270 _____ ($.15 \times 1,800 = 270$)

   f. Check your answer. If you got an incorrect answer, tell how you know it is wrong. Then write the correct answer.

      Students who got incorrect answers should mention computation error or

      that the answer was not reasonable.

7. Gary bought a pair of boots and 3 pairs of socks for $41. The boots cost $35. How much did *each* pair of socks cost?
   a. Underline the question.
   b. Circle the needed facts in the problem.

   c. Describe your plan: __Subtract and divide (total cost − cost of boots = cost of 3 pairs of socks; cost of 3 pairs of socks ÷ 3 = cost of 1 pair of socks)__

   d. If an estimate can be made, show it here: __40 − 35 = 5; 6 ÷ 3 = 2__

   e. Carry out your plan. Answer: __$2.00__   (41 − 35 = 6; 6 ÷ 3 = 2)

   f. Check your answer. If you got an incorrect answer, tell how you know it is wrong. Then write the correct answer.

   __Students who got incorrect answers should mention computation error or__

   __that the answer was not reasonable.__

8. Fran invested $5,000 at 6% simple interest for $2\frac{1}{2}$ years. How much interest did she earn?
   a. Underline the question.
   b. Circle the needed facts in the problem.

   c. Describe your plan: __Use a formula. (i = prt)__

   d. If an estimate can be made, show it here: __5,000 × .06 × 3 = 900__

   e. Carry out your plan. Answer: __$750__   (5,000 × .06 × 2.5 = 750)

   f. Check your answer. If you got an incorrect answer, tell how you know it is wrong. Then write the correct answer.

   __Students who got incorrect answers should mention computation error or__

   __that the answer was not reasonable.__

This is the end of the Whole-Book Review.

Appendix

Table of Measures

Metric System		Customary System

Length

Metric System	Customary System
10 millimeters (mm) = 1 centimeter (cm)	12 inches (in.) = 1 foot (ft.)
10 centimeters / 100 millimeters } = 1 decimeter (dm)	3 feet / 36 inches } = 1 yard (yd.)
10 decimeters / 100 centimeters } = 1 meter (m)	1,760 yards / 5,280 feet } = 1 mile (mi.)
1,000 meters = 1 kilometer (km)	6,076 feet = 1 nautical mile

Area

Metric System	Customary System
100 square millimeters (mm²) = 1 square centimeter (cm²)	144 square inches (sq. in.) = 1 square foot (sq. ft.)
10,000 square centimeters = 1 square meter (m²)	9 square feet = 1 square yard (sq. yd.)
100 square meters = 1 are (a)	4,840 square yards = 1 acre (A.)
10,000 square meters = 1 hectare (ha)	640 acres = 1 square mile (sq. mi.)

Volume

Metric System	Customary System
1,000 cubic millimeters (mm³) = 1 cubic centimeter (cm³)	1,728 cubic inches (cu. in.) = 1 cubic foot (cu. ft.)
1,000 cubic centimeters = 1 cubic decimeter (dm³)	27 cubic feet = 1 cubic yard (cu. yd.)
1,000,000 cubic centimeters = 1 cubic meter (m³)	

Mass/Weight

Metric System	Customary System
1,000 milligrams (mg) = 1 gram (g)	16 ounces (oz.) = 1 pound (lb.)
1,000 grams = 1 kilogram (kg)	2,000 pounds = 1 ton (T.)
1,000 kilograms = 1 metric ton (t)	

Capacity

Metric System	Customary System
1,000 milliliters (mL) = 1 liter (L)	8 fluid ounces (fl. oz.) = 1 cup (c.)
	2 cups = 1 pint (pt.)
	2 pints = 1 quart (qt.)
	4 quarts = 1 gallon (gal.)

Time

60 seconds = 1 minute	365 days		
60 minutes = 1 hour	52 weeks } = 1 year		
24 hours = 1 day	12 months		
7 days = 1 week	366 days = 1 leap year		

Operations Chart

Action	Operation
Joining different-sized groups (a different number in each group) to find a total	Addition
Separating Objects to find a group that is left or **Comparing two groups** to find the difference	Subtraction
Joining equal groups to find a total	Multiplication
Sharing equally to find the size of each group or **Making groups of a given size** to find the number of groups	Division

Geometric Formulas

square — s (side)

rectangle — w (width), l (length)

triangle — h (height), b (base)

parallelogram — h (height), b (base)

circle — d (diameter), r (radius)

rectangular prism — h (height), w (width), l (length)

Other Formulas

distance = rate × time, or $d = rt$

interest = principal × rate × time, or $i = prt$

unit price = $\dfrac{\text{total cost}}{\text{number of units}}$

probability = $\dfrac{\text{number of favorable outcomes}}{\text{number of possible outcomes}}$

sales tax = rate of sales tax × price of item

total cost = price + sales tax

discount = rate of discount × original price

sale price = original price − discount

total pay = regular pay + overtime pay